T0195094

Suit Your Self

A Study Guide to Learning How to Read the Plain Deck of Cards

ELIZABETH MELO, MHS. M

BALBOA.
PRESS
A DIVISION OF HAY HOUSE

Balboa Press books may be ordered through booksellers or by contacting:

Balboa Press
A Division of Hay House
1663 Liberty Drive
Bloomington, IN 47403
www.balboapress.com
1 (877) 407-4847

Because of the dynamic nature of the Internet, any web addresses or links contained in this book may have changed since publication and may no longer be valid. The views expressed in this work are solely those of the author and do not necessarily reflect the views of the publisher, and the publisher hereby disclaims any responsibility for them.

The author of this book does not dispense medical advice or prescribe the use of any technique as a form of treatment for physical, emotional, or medical problems without the advice of a physician, either directly or indirectly. The intent of the author is only to offer information of a general nature to help you in your quest for emotional and spiritual well-being. In the event you use any of the information in this book for yourself, which is your constitutional right, the author and the publisher assume no responsibility for your actions.

Any people depicted in stock imagery provided by Getty Images are models, and such images are being used for illustrative purposes only. Certain stock imagery © Getty Images.

Print information available on the last page.

ISBN: 978-1-9822-3337-2 (sc)
ISBN: 978-1-9822-3338-9 (e)

Balboa Press rev. date: 08/20/2019

About the Author

Elizabeth Melo is a painter, writer and intuitive. She demonstrated unique insight from a very early age while developing her first passion, which was writing poetry. At age 12, she was fascinated by Astrology and Philosophy.

Since then, Elizabeth has studied Metaphysics, specializing in Hypnosis and Holistic Life Coaching/Spiritual Counselling, and intends to continue her studies in the field of Anomalous Research and Paranormal Science. She is a member of the International Metaphysical Practitioners Association, and a Minister of the International Society of Metaphysical Humanism, Inc. (ISoMH). She has also studied Reiki, various meditation techniques and is a passionate student of philosophy.

Elizabeth has been providing readings to clients for over 30 years using both plain deck and Tarot cards. She is life-long Mystic dedicated to both living her truth and inspiring others to do the same.

Welcome

Many times I have been asked how a small plain deck of cards can bring so much clarity to one's life. Finally, as I put the kettle on for a steaming hot cuppa tea with the last lingering rays of sunlight slowly creeping its way across the table, it reminds me that it's the end of the day and the time of dusk and dreams begin. I notice the gathering shadows as I reach for pen and paper while the day slips into the night and I turn on the lights and chase away the shadows. I laugh out loud when I realize the ironic symbolism of chasing away the shadows that shrouds the method of Divination called Cartomancy and begin to write the way to demystify the questions that so many have asked.

This book is designed to answer the multitude of questions that I have been asked over the many years of providing card readings and psychic guidance to individuals around the world. No matter where the seeker comes from, their age or their gender, they come with questions, not just about their own lives and future but about my life, experiences and gifts. Sometimes they approach with a sense of scepticism and disbelief, determined to prove that it is merely astute students of human psychology and body language, that those of us that are gifted have in fact deluded ourselves into believing we possess "special powers". Others seem somewhat awestruck, harbouring their own illusions of demi-gods, endowed with magic, super powers or are privy to personal, spiritual guidance. No matter if they come as curious sceptics or true believers, they come armed with as many questions about readers and the mysteries of divination as they do about what the future holds for them.

This book is an attempt to answer these many questions, taking the art of Cartomancy from the mysterious shadows or circus side shows and bringing it into the illuminating light of day. By dismissing the myths and illusions about who readers are, and what they do, it dispels the image of a magician, charlatan or prophet and expose card readers for what they really are... *ordinary* people who have developed and nurtured a *natural* talent that exists within each of us. No magic! No mumbo jumbo! Just hard work, study and confidence in human instinct.

This book is written two-fold: it serves as a tool for those who wish to benefit more from the readings they seek from others; but it also may inspire and instruct those who wish to develop their own intuition and embark on a journey of self-discovery that leads to greater confidence, better decision making and ultimately their ability to take the role as reader as well as seeker.

Although the art of Cartomancy is neither
magic nor mystery,
it is however magical and mysterious.

This may seem a contradiction but it is very accurate. The magical part is the discovery of your own hidden gifts, like picking up a guitar for the first time and discovering you can make beautiful music. The mysterious part is nothing more than the unwillingness *or* inability of those who have developed the gift to impart that knowledge to others. There are those who treat the art of divination like it is a trade secret, afraid to dispel the illusion of their personal power. Others would gladly share but lack the ability to articulate their knowledge to others, not unlike those that can play the guitar but cannot teach another how to play.

After many years of questions, here is the knowledge and understanding of what is truly one of mankind's greatest yet most undeveloped *natural* gifts. Join me as we chase away the shadows and share a spiritual adventure that will amaze and enlighten you.

The kettle is whistling...shall we begin?

"My teachings are easy to understand
and easy to put into practice."

Yet your intellect will never grasp them,
and if you try to practice them, you will fail.

My teachings are older than the world.
How can you grasp their meaning?

If you want to know me, look inside your heart.
~ Lao Tzu

Learning to Read a Plain Deck Cards!

Do you want to learn how to read the plain deck of cards?

Cartomancy is fun and exciting, and can assist you and others in self-discovery and to capture a glimpse of what the future might hold. A reading through Cartomancy provides guidance, for your life, your choices, your potential, in love, career, and life goals. It touches on the past, present, and the future.

> *I am always doing what I cannot do yet,*
> *in order to learn how to do it." ~ Vincent Van Gogh*

Cartomancy is the use of a standard deck of 52 playing cards plus two jokers. This ancient medium is chosen for several reasons:

- Universal Elements: The art of Cartomancy makes use of techniques, skills and symbols that are used in almost every other form of divination. Understanding the basics of Cartomancy will provide you with a firm foundation to build upon should you wish to explore other avenues of divination later. Meditation, numerology, symbolism, and the development of instinctual awareness are just a few of the elements of Cartomancy that you will find useful in understanding other divinatory methods.

- Familiarity: Most people are familiar with at least the basic suits and symbols. In fact, without even knowing it, you are already familiar with many of the meanings through common superstitions and historical references. You are already partway there!

- Cost and availability: They can be purchased at any discount or dollar store for a buck or two! The gift of personal insight should not be the right of the rich only!

- Common usage: It is one of the most frequently used methods for divination in North America.

- Flexibility: This method can be personalized depending on the seeker, their question or circumstance.

- Specific information provided: Although intuition is still required the cards provide more *specific* information to assist you then other methods. Cards are the vehicle that expresses information, and intuition is your ability to drive. Some methods require much study and practise before you will glean any results. With Cartomancy you experience greater success as you *begin* your journey and are thus more likely to continue and perfect your technique over time.

The bottom line is that you will enjoy the guidance that the cards will provide and over time you will master their meaning.

The most important thing to remember is that there is no fixed future, and free will is forever our human right.

Each reading should be taken from the point of view that each moment is not predetermined, and can change according to how we respond to the current situations. That is why we often say "forewarned is forearmed", which is to say that we hold all the power to determine our own future, and the ability to change that version of the future still lies within each of us.

*"If you do not change direction,
you may end up where you are heading"
~ Tao Tzu*

Elizabeth Melo, MHs. M

What is Cartomancy?

Cartomancy is the truest form of divination that symbolizes the Gypsy fortune telling, and so easy to learn. Much like the Tarot Deck, without the major arcana, the numbers and suits have specific meanings.

With some dedication and time to learn the meanings of individual cards, and then to combine the meanings together, anyone can learn the art of Cartomancy. Here you will find within these pages the meaning of each of the four suits: *Clubs, Hearts, Diamonds and Spades*. You will learn the meaning of each card, and spreads for you to practice. There will also be example readings and their interpretation. The more you practice the more the cards will communicate with you through the spirit of symbols and sublime messages.

When learning the interpretation of individual cards, there will also be a word or phrase association which will make it easier to memorize the cards. Most important is to follow your instincts and apply your own interpretations as you go along. Explore the power of your mind and let your own word association come through. Be comfortable and relax.

Initially when you start, take some time and shuffle the cards, cut the deck several times and just keep your mind blank. By doing this your energy will flow through the cards.

Take the meanings of the cards first and then use word recaps association, and you will naturally expand on their meanings as you go along. You will also find it easier to memorize them once you have broken down the meanings.

Intuition

There are those who would declare that psychic ability and divination are completely unscientific. They will trot out the standard arguments about being unable to produce results and the inability to measure it in an unbiased manner. However, we must resign ourselves to the fact that humanity's lack of knowledge to measure something does not contradict its existence.

> *The lack of an equation to express it did not mean that gravity did not exist before Isaac Newton.*

Our inability to see and measure micro-organisms certainly did nothing to diminish their realism and effects on humanity prior to the invention of the first microscope.

> *"Men build too many walls, and not enough bridges"*
> *~ Isaac Newton*

In most discussions on psychic phenomena and divination there is no differentiation between scientific methods. It has become increasingly accepted that scientific validity is based on the *experimental method;* the ability to provide measurable data that can be reproduced within a controlled environment. These are the methods used by modern micro-biology and medicine to study germs and disease as well as the methods used by physicists to explain the laws of gravity and many other laws of physics.

Most people however, do not realize that it was *empirical methods* that lead to the discovery of those methods of measurement. Empirical research is the collection of large amounts of data without knowing what it necessarily means or what it is for. It is the method that has traditionally been used to enter into a study of previously unexplored fields. Ironically, empirical research by its very nature requires a higher level of intuition then other forms of scientific research. As we increase our base of empirical data on divination and psychic ability it will help us move to a more experimental method of exploration and hopefully at some point result in the development of a reliable method of measuring and explaining psychic phenomena.

No great discovery was every made without a bold guess.
~ Isaac Newton

All science starts with the most ancient of science – metaphysics, combining the spirit with science, it starts with a question!

This book is written as a practical method while promoting no particular theology. In my many years of experience, the truth is that ***intention is the purest form of any action***. It can be manifested through religion, science or magic or your own pure desire. If you put your intention out there, so to speak, then it is reciprocated. The experience is both science and magic. Fundamentally that's nature.

"Nature is pleased with simplicity. And Nature is no dummy"
~ Isaac Newton

Cultivating our intuition is exploring ideas with an open mind, setting our intention, and most of all developing how we see ourselves and the world around us.

Divination

Psychic phenomena has excited many since ancient times. Through history many of the greatest leaders and famous influential people of the world have consulted psychics.

Despite the controversy surrounding divination, it is still a popular practice to consult psychics in matters of life, death, career, love and family. Being psychic allows the skill of perceiving events that are yet unknown, whether they relate to the past, present or future. It's the interaction of all three related to your life. The part of the past that relates to the present and the future, is the likely part of the past that will arise during a reading.

The difference between a *seeker* - the person seeking a reading, and the psychic *reader* - the person providing the reading, is that the latter has developed the capacity to deliberately sense the energy radiated by each individual. Traditionally, spiritualists have believed that everything is made up of energy that vibrates, and that energy radiates through each of us. This energy releases signals, messages, and emotions. The psychic has learned to harness the gift of readings these messages through the use of divination as the tool, much like a vehicle and the psychic reader as the driver.

Reading energy for psychics is a natural skill, however the ability to read energy is innate within us all. Through practice, learning this divination method, listening to your inner voice, and trusting in your natural gift, you can use the cards to guide you and others along life's path.

"Study the past, if you would divine the future."
~ Confucius

Elizabeth Melo, MHs. M

When learning the art of divination, in this case Cartomancy, there are some important points to consider:

1. ***Most people who practice any form of psychic phenomena or divination are aware that a strict code of ethics is required.*** They are fully aware of the energy implications, and thus they most often use the art in the most profound and logical reasoning after careful and conscious deliberation on universal energy. This is often theorized as combining the divine power with the source of earth energy, however, its true intent comes from the energy of the person subjectively seeking a psychic reading. Here, we must bear in mind, with the Laws of Karma in place, a tooth for a tooth, an eye for an eye, we should choose wisely, and reflect the love of universe in all that we do. *You are responsible for your actions, and the reaction of energy that unfolds.*

2. ***Life is like a wave, growing and changing and crashing and starting all over again, its perpetual motion is constant.*** If you are giving a reading then take heed to the expression that *'some things are better left unsaid'* and that there is always a light to be found in the darkness. Remember that a card reading can be taken very seriously, and it can devastate a seeker, leaving a person distraught and deflated. When reading this should be kept in mind, and as a reader, our words must be chosen wisely, and in deep consideration of the other person.

"Remember not only to say the right thing in the right place, but far more difficult still, to leave unsaid the wrong thing at the tempting moment." ~ Benjamin Franklin

3. ***The most important thing to remember is that absolutely nothing over powers the will of human-kind, our free will.*** It is within our power to form our destiny. The information presented in readings is meant only to provide guidance; it is not written in stone. The power to change our destiny always

remains with our choices. The most gifted readers are cognisant of this fact and are fully aware of the laws of karma. Having a reading or consultation should help you understand your alternatives and not dictate an absolute destiny. The power of free will is forever present. Nothing can take away your power to choose.

A strong code of ethics includes privacy, compassion, non-judgment and honesty. If you are learning to develop your intuition and practice divination, you should exercise sincerity and be concerned about the quality of the reading and how it may psychologically and emotionally impact the seeker.

The Rippling Effect is energy in transition. Energy affects us and those around us, and permeates our surroundings. This is cause and effect. Those affected by us, begin to affect others and so on. In the effort of expanding positive energy, we could begin to shape life and all that exists. *It's a beautiful concept! Live it! Breathe it!*

"To every action there is always opposed and equal reaction." ~ Isaac Newton

In order to shape our mental power we need to consistently work on changing our inner attitude. We can use visualization, affirmation and meditation to transform our thought process. When we feel negative thoughts surface, work on changing them, make it our priority to reconstruct our mind frame. It can take some time to master our way of thinking, but it is most rewarding in the end. Harmonizing our spirit leads to the chain action + the reaction to materializing a better universe. That which we attract!

During a reading, we are in essence exchanging energy with another person. We have the power to change our destiny by changing our energy frequency. Nothing, I mean absolutely nothing, over powers our free will.

Elizabeth Melo, MHs. M

We are masters of our own destiny.

In my experience, the most important reason that people seek out a reading is validation. Yes, its true people are looking for answers, direction, and hope, but validation, in itself, empowers us to take action.

A reading provides people with the opportunity to let out suppressed thoughts and feelings, without saying a word. Hearing an outside version of our feelings articulated by an objective source can help us understand our sense of truth, or can help understand the outside influences that affect our lives. Validation gives each one of us meaning, the significance of what is happening, and what will arise as a result, but also allows us to see the choices that govern the reading.

Happiness is... when you participate in your own life!

A card reading should be an empowering experience and help the seeker gain perspective on current events in their life, aid in calming the storm and provide guidance. The ultimate answers lie in the seeker's choices, made through their own free will.

The Way of Science

As I stated earlier on, metaphysics is the beginning stages of all science. All you have to do is hold a question! That is the seed that germinates the investigation, leading to the evidence that proves or disproves a theory.

However, take for example, perpetual motion that has been baffling science since the invention of the wheel. In 1712, Johann Bessler invented a self-moving wheel that was locked away for a period of time, and when unlocked, the device was still turning. Science was unable to explain the phenomena, so it began to discredit the invention. Since it has neither been proven nor disproven how it was invented, perpetual motion remains to this day as an 'impossibility.

On the flip side, Galileo Galilei, the father of modern science and a religious man, made the discovery that the sun, and in fact not the earth, was the centre of the universe. He discovered that it lay motionlessly, while the earth and other planets rotated the sun. Unfortunately, his claim was seen as an attempt to defile the bible, and he was accused of hearsay by the church, which led to spending the last of his days under house arrest.

*"Facts which at first seem improbable will,
even on scant explanation, drop the cloak which
has hidden them and stand forth in naked and simple beauty"
~ Galileo Galilei*

Science has yet to explain psychic phenomena, but nonetheless it exists and unexplained evidence is everywhere.

Elizabeth Melo, MHs. M

If we set aside our skepticism, and for a moment consider the evidence with an open mind and forget the "how", we can discover humankind's greatest gift.

Introducing myself, I would say I am just as much of a believer as I am a skeptic. For every new idea that arises, I place it under my own scrutiny, I ponder deeply, I contemplate and meditate, consider the evidence and eventually I come to the conclusion of whether it resonates with my truth. I consider science, deep personal belief systems regardless of its origin and seek out answers.

Therefore I would say that I believe in both science and magic, yet I question both, and I do not consider them mutually exclusive but in fact two sides of the same coin.

Metaphysics, which is applying the laws of nature, not only harmonizes with traditional science, it is science and spirituality combined. Only when we experience something for ourselves can we find the answers that are within us. How many times did you think of something only to have it spoken of shortly thereafter, or to think of a person, and that person reaches out. It is through our own experiences that we can gather evidence, albeit without scientific approval. It is our boundaries that restrict our natural fibre. By placing our reservations aside, letting go of our preconceived notions, social acceptance, and embedded beliefs we can discover our greatest gift.

Collecting and exploring all possibilities, considering fact and knowledge, and devotion to our inner voice, is the core of true wisdom.

*"Magic is believing in yourself,
if you can do that, you can make anything happen."
Johann Wolfgang von Geothe*

Natural Power

Of course we all have heard of the positive thinking new age wave! It's everywhere! The human race begins to work towards manifesting their dreams. Do we define this as Magic, and what is Magic?

Breaking it down to super-NATURAL power!
Natural as in our nature and our own capability!

Our birth right.
Enchanting and mysterious? Yes! But very, very natural!

I try to explain to my clients that this enchanting magic is all about energy, and the interconnection involved in creating power between all frequencies. The manifestation of positive thoughts, visualization and the power of affirmation, which is repetitive thinking on positive statements supposedly sent out into the universe, is intended so that the universe will respond.

Many people practice prayer in hopes of achieving their desires and wishes, asking God to help them. Prayer, by its definition is a solemn request or a thanks giving to God, Goddess or other object of worship. Regardless, it is our effort to communicate with a higher power. For me personally, Gratitude is the root of my beliefs.

The miracles that arise from affirmation, visualization, or consistent prayer are often attributed to a super-*Natural* power. Metaphysics interprets this as all *Natural*, wielding our true power – and this of course is our free will.

Nothing over powers our free will, we have the ability to choose. Although having a reading done is considered a guide to understanding the path we are on, it does not mean we cannot change the direction.

Learning to meditate creates a level of concentration that encourage us to understand our energy and the energy of the universe. When we master meditation, we learn to focus the mind and build energy strength. It is mastering this ability to work our energy that creates our successes and failures.

Ultimately, how we think is critical, positive attracts positive, negative attracts negative. Much like those who refer to Karma!

In other words think of Karma
as not punishment for our action,
but the earned energy frequency we have created.

The Power of the subconscious interconnects the natural forces, and the laws of attraction, enforced by the energy that interacts throughout the universe.

Metaphysics, approached from a more philosophical point of view, it is the open minded review of wisdom and truth, the discipline of how we live, listening to our true nature, and applying the principles of reasoning as the very foundations of our existence. The will of our intention is the sum of both nature and energy.

Our pre-conditioning can often interfere in our expanding consciousness, by super imposed social belief, family traditions, politics, religion, etc. However logic is a gift that allows us to have the ability for reasoning. Learning depends upon ourselves, explore logically our inner guidance and intuition, and it is important to our personal growth and to the act of living free.

It takes practice to pay attention to our intuition, balance our logical thinking with our soul energy to identify truth, but it is a blessing that guides us throughout every avenue of our lives.

After all, following our spiritual nature is equally as important as following our human nature. It is the duality of human-kind!

Universal Energy

With Quantum Physics, we have come to learn that energy can be manipulated, that energy effects energy, and are part of the universal all! This breaks down to all things are interconnected by the same energy. We are born to free will and the power of choice to abide by our own order. The decisions we make supply the cause of effect.

It is exciting to know that Science has proven that we are pure energy! We are made of molecules that further break down to atoms, but if you further break down the atoms, all you are left with is energy. If all energy is interconnected, and energy can be manipulated, it can also be understood.

"Science does not know its debt to imagination."
~ Ralph Waldo Emerson

When reading cards we are interconnecting energy, as part of a collective. We do this every day without realizing that we are. It is our human condition. Have you ever noticed that when one person is having a good day, so are many others, and the same for bad days. Often there is nothing related to the occurrence, and this energy supersedes distance. Facebook shows us this amazing phenomena. One person states they are having a wonderful day, the next thing you know so are a dozen other people from all over the globe. Watching this energy in affect is miraculous.

We should not to be clouded by our need to
intellectually understand our existence,
we are more than that.
We must combine our logic with our instinct
to be true to ourselves.

De-Mystifying the Process

Developing your intuition is perhaps the greatest gift you can give to yourself. Learning to listen to and trust your first instincts can lead to greater success in every area of life including career and finances, personal relationships, romance and family and even health.

Trusting our instincts can even help avoid those seemingly random events that we so often see as being beyond our control. Perhaps you couldn't *stop* the tornado that careens at you at 200mph but perhaps you could have avoided it had you listened to that little voice that, for no apparent reason, told you to turn left rather than right!

How often do we wish we had followed our hunch? How much better off we would have been if we had listened to our instinct? Why do we so quickly dismiss our quiet inner voice?

This is the language of intuitively accessing information beyond the limitation of our five senses.

Intuition is a natural law that all people possess. Intuition is our birth right, and one of our less explored senses.

You can learn to master your ability to access energy. Learning the skill of intuition can help you in the daily process of life. It's about following that hunch, or listening to that feeling. The happiest people in the world are the people who listen actively to their first initial feeling. By listening to our hunch, we are listening to our higher power. Our connection to this power is the communication channel of life.

You can develop your psychic ability by understanding what it means and practicing some very simple techniques. As we move into a new era of the open mind and the yearning for answers, a new generation of unlimited spiritual development and psychic ability can give you the guidance to your true creative powers. The greatest power is within. Suddenly, you will find that the un-explainable becomes clear.

When you examine the potential of energy, and explore the affects that energy has in your personal space, you can learn how energy affects you on a daily basis, and by this observation, you can learn to read energy and control how it affects you on a personal and psychic level. Every person has the ability to affect their own energy. Most people have had some experiences which they don't understand. A sudden knowing, a flash of intuition or a feeling, that does not appear rational at that very moment but becomes obvious to us with the passing of time. How often do you hear people say: "I knew that", "I had a feeling", "My gut said" and so on. They are experiencing intuition at work.

In today's world of practical, material foreplay which entices our physical senses, we forget to pay attention to what surrounds us, the energy at work, the beauty of nature, the splendor of color and the conjuring of music. Ultimately we forget to pay attention to our spiritual selves.

We jeopardize our very essence and deny our deeper senses. Unable to distinguish between intellect vs. emotion vs. intuition, the mysterious undertone of the inexplicable knowing is too often ignored by our primitive material nature.

By building the bridge from your material nature to your true energy, you can learn to expand upon your own gift or at least understand and respect the gifts of others, especially when they so readily share them with you. Today, people seek out guidance either through readings or spiritual healing, and the shared objective is to understand our lives and our selves better.

*In time, you begin clearing the path way
to grounding your energy.*

We can then grasp that there is a linkage of energy between us all, and that we communicate and exchange a hidden dynamism, then it makes sense that readings are a reflection of intuition, which is energy in motion.

All methods of extra-sensory ability require the gift of sensing energy, outside of scientific measurement. Interpretation is the ability to read energy at will, by being responsive to the energy of the seeker. You can learn to expand upon your intuition, by discipline, mediation, research and practice. If you open to the understanding of your abilities and discover your skills of listening to your "gut instinct", you will capture the ability that lies within you. The ability that lies within us all!

*Sometimes I drive to chase the sunset.
The sunsets of my life have been bittersweet,
as the sun disappears,
there is a promise it will rise one again.
I grapple to find my truth in this beauty.
I have been chasing my sunsets,
and holding on to its generous wisdom,
for nature understands me better than I do.*

Elizabeth Melo, MHs. M

Developing the Gift of Intuition?

To one degree or another we all have intuition and it varies from person to person. It is important to remember that the material world has dulled our senses, and this can jeopardize our spiritual self. We have become lethargic about our instinct, but it's time to reawaken so that we can embrace the natural gifts bestowed on each of us.

> *I do not feel obliged to believe that the same God who has endowed us with sense, reason, and intellect has intended us to forgo their use. ~ Galileo Galilei*

Today with the new age movement rolling forward quickly, people are becoming open to all the possibilities. But remember that turning blind faith over to new age is no different than blind faith to any other belief structure. ***You must believe in yourself!*** Appreciate the simple beauty in life, and embrace your nature, within and without. This is the time of forward thinking. Not advanced thinking but... returning to who we really are, and no longer should we deny our true and divine nature. True forward thinking is more ancient then new age.

1. Meditation: One of the best ways to increase your intuition and develop psychic ability is through meditation. Today, you can purchase books, or go on the internet to learn about this skill. Meditation increases your ability to concentrate, teach you to listen to your inner voice, as well as your body, mind and spirit. Balancing all three through mediation gives us deep guidance and self-healing wellness.

Meditation can break barriers of social belief that instill preconceived ideas from time of birth to present day, instilled in us by our families, society, and organized groups. Breaking down these beliefs begins by opening your spirit to new ideas and possibilities. By removing these boundaries, you will begin to hear your true voice, the limitless spirit beyond horizon, beyond the five senses and beyond social pre-conceived notions that have placed rigid limitations on your ability to see beyond the mind and listen to the energy in motion flowing all around us.

2. Hypnosis: Or more specifically self-hypnosis – is more like a guided meditation. It is a subliminal message being sent into the superconscious mind and can have a remarkable effect on our lives. Hypnosis has many astonishing benefits such as reducing stress, pain management, modifying behavior, breaking hindering habits, build self-confidence, instill mindfulness, overcome our fears and attune our energy. Not only will you experience a peace surrounding you, but you will also become more alert to the energy around you.

Ideally you can create your own hypnosis recording, however to start, you will find there are several hypnosis recordings available on line. Choose them according to your needs, as they are often designed for a specific purpose. Some people use self-hypnosis to overcome additions, face their deepest fairs, or just to gain some confidence. There is a whole list of other resources you will find.

"What hurts this person is not the occurrence itself,
for another person might not feel oppressed
by this situation at all.
What is hurting this person is the response
he or she has uncritically adopted.
It is not a demonstration of kindness or friendship
to the people we care about to join them in indulging

in wrongheaded, negative feelings."
~ Epictetus,

3. Radio Dial: Sensing energy resembles listening to the radio. If the dial keeps twirling around, then there is no specific vibration being transmitted. In other words, it's all over the place and you cannot interpret the messages. In order to listen to the radio, you need to set the dial on one particular station, fine tuning to a specific energy. This is the duty of the Reader, to attune to the energy of a Seeker. The wave lengths emanated from each seeker is the same analogy, and the psychic is the tuning system. Being attuned to radio energy is learning to tap into one specific frequency at a time.

    Try experimenting with the concept of radio dial energy. Sit with a mirror in a quiet place. Make sure that you have soft lighting, or for maximum effect burning candles. For several moments stare into your own reflection, specifically focused on your third eye, the center of your forehead. Try not to blink too much. Concentrate on your breathing, taking slow deep breaths and exhale completely. As you do this make note of what you see and how you feel. Do you see changes in your reflection? Eventually you can experience seeing your own energy around your body as you practice. It may have color, or might just be a soft glow of clear light. Try recording your experiences and see how it evolves for you. In time and with practice you will begin to see energy at will, even begin to see the energy around objects, and other people without the aid of this experiment.

4. Aura: This brings us to our Aura, which is the energy field around your body, and often it is a rainbow of colors vibrating according to mood, health, and our Chakras, which are energy vortexes held within the body. Reiki or healing touch is a form of energy healing through the aura. However, aura does not

only surround people, it is also present around and objects. It is faithfully everywhere.

Much like Radio Dial, you can practice seeing your own aura in the mirror. Make sure that behind you there is nothing but a blank canvas that will not interfere with the imagery, such as shadows that can be created or other objects. Stare or focus deeply on the center of the forehead where it is said your third eye is located. Your gaze should remain here and try to blink as little as possible. If at first you still find it really hard to see anything, squint your eyes a little until you have mastered it a little more. Stay focused, and in time it will get easier and you will be able to see energy at will, anytime and in any lighting.

"We cannot teach people anything;
we can only help them discover it within themselves."
~ Galileo Galilei

5. Psychometry: This is the ability to sense energy by holding an object and capturing its story, and who the object is attached to. Through meditation and enhanced concentration you can learn read an object.

    Personally I use psychometry during a reading. I hold an object belonging to the seeker, likely a piece of jewelry, while I do the reading. This helps me connect to the person, while I am reading and receiving impressions, or images.

6. Emotional intention: It is paramount to learn how to keep emotions in check. Passion and other emotions, along with attitude are central to giving a good reading. Since giving a reading is about the seeker, you cannot allow your personal feelings to interfere with the quality of a reading. When giving a reading try to be impartial and open to anything that comes

to mind, whether you agree or disagree with a person's thoughts, life style, or general being. In order to be open, you must set boundaries on our own emotions, the very emotions that restrict our capacities and talents. You can learn to do this with meditation, and practicing an open mind is just a better way to live.

Keep your attention focused entirely on what is
truly your own concern, and be clear that
what belongs to others is their business and none of yours.
~ Epictetus

7. Impressions vs. Thoughts: When our emotions get in the way, we are less likely to understand the difference between our thoughts and impressions. Thoughts have everything to do with being personal, while impressions are quick flashes of intuition. When we think too much, it interferes with our impressions, which is to say that first initial feeling or vision. Sometimes they do not make sense to us personally but make sense to the seeker. Once you understand the difference, you can start paying attention to your impressions.

8. Attitude: Have the right attitude! If you really want to learn how to read cards, then believe in yourself, and practice various ways to increase your intuition. Remember, intention, in its self is very important. Place your intention on what you want to achieve and you will. With an open mind, you can have endless possibilities with your intuition. Even if you simply want to hear your inner voice, or initial feeling to help with your everyday problems, it can be very useful. It truly is a difficult task to change how you have been taught to see, feel, think and react. We have learned from our parents, society, teachers, friends and possibility stringent belief systems to shape ourselves as they have instructed, but the truth is you are you, and you can

change anything. The most wonderful part of having an open mind is that you can begin to see things through your own eyes, so to speak.

It cannot be expressed enough the personal freedom you will feel when not chained to preconditioning, but ready to explore possibilities without restriction. The truth is inside each one of us; all we have to do is look more deeply.

9. Practice: It is important to remember that intuition is like a muscle that requires development, practice, and exercise regularly. Over time you will develop your own way to increasing your intuition.

> *It vexes me when they would constrain science*
> *by the authority of the Scriptures, and yet*
> *do not consider themselves bound to*
> *answer reason and experiment.* ~ Galileo

Elizabeth Melo, MHs. M

Ways to Practice Intuition

Now you know how to develop your intuition, here are a few suggested ways to practice the development of your instinct. If you keep practicing it will amaze you how connected you begin to feel to others, and more importantly how you connect to yourself.

All that we are is a result of what we thought.
The mind is everything.
What we think, we become. ~ Buddha

1. Take a deck of cards and shuffle them well. Take a few deep breaths, and begin from the top of the deck, going through card by card, and begin concentrating on the color and suit before you turn it over. Remember that you are following your very first impression. Form three piles, one for the correct color and suit, one of the correct color, and one for those you did not get correctly. This is often best done with someone else, as you can be thrown off by your logical thought process. For example if you see hearts four times in a row, it doesn't make logical sense that the fifth card could be a heart as well. However, you are learning to follow your first instinct, and avoid logical choice.

2. Take a five minute break, two or three times a day, to focus on one simple thing. It can be a fly in the room, it can be nick in the wall, or the shape of your coffee cup. It takes very little time, but a great amount of discipline and it can help increase your attention and concentration. For those who have difficulty in learning to meditate this is particularly good. You will be surprised that some will not make it through the five minutes at first. Don't worry, all in good time. What you will learn from

this exercise is just how unfocused you really are on a day to day basis.

3. Stop living life on auto-pilot. Pay more attention to your routine and the little things you do throughout the day. We do so much unconsciously, and commonly we depend on familiarity way too much. You run to the sock drawer and you put them on, without a single thought. You wash dishes without really paying attention to what you are doing. The list goes on and on, but if you begin to pay more attention to these little things, you begin to pay more attention to the much bigger things. As a little tip, this helps us to not take things for granted so much, and be more grateful for all the little things that make life easier.

Lao Tzu once said
"A journey to a thousand miles begins with one single step."

This inspires me to keep moving, keeping guessing,
and keep discovering!

Elizabeth Melo, MHs. M

Learning to Read Cards!

You want to learn how to read the plain deck of cards! Cartomancy is fun and exciting, and can assist you and others in self-discovery and to capture a glimpse of the future.

Little by little over time, it will become easy and second nature. There are few tips you can do to help you learn the Cartomancy.

1. Start with small readings. Take the cards and examine how they relate to your life and question. Try to be objective.

2. Journal your readings. Write the date, the cards and a brief meaning, this will allow you to refer back but also retain card meanings.

3. Your Daily Reading is by far the best way to learn to read cards. Start each day with a small spread, and decipher its meaning according to what you anticipate for the day. By doing a journal each day you can review it once a week to determine how it fit into your life and record your results.

4. Keep the word association list available in this book as a quick reference. It will help you remember the full interpretations that I encourage you will learn first.

5. Practice, practice, practice! By doing a spread each day you will begin to remember what the cards mean and how they intertwine with each other.

The most important lesson I have learned in a life time of reading cards for myself and others, is to not take myself or life too seriously.

I dare you to - have fun, enjoy and explore.

The Essence of Suits & Numbers

At first glance when you lay out the cards in a spread, there are two important things to consider, first and foremost is to understand the suits. *Is there a dominate suit in the spread?* Each suit corresponds to distinct areas of a person's life.

Once you understand what each suit represents, it can give you an overview synopsis of the readings. The essence of the governing suit will give an overall assessment of the main topic on the mind of the seeker.

The second consideration to give during your synopsis is the number sequence. *Is there a particular number that is repeating?* Echoing numbers also give a reference or warning in a reading.

The dominating suits and repetitive numbers will set the tone for the reading and is a good place to start with your interpretations. I find it helpful to get a vibe going right from the start, because once you start, it opens a gateway and information begins to flood through, and with practice this will both amaze and delight you.

Once you have captured the overall essence, you can begin breaking down the meanings according to their position in the spread, and their individual interpretation.

Let your spirit dance
in the eminence of your perception.

Capture the quintessence of the heart
and learn that the truth to be found
is not quantified by knowledge,
but the quality of wisdom.

Hearts

Key word or phrase:
Matters of the Heart

Hearts represent matters dealing with the Heart. It speaks to emotional matters, and symbolizes love, all types of relationships, the deepest hopes and celebrations, but it can also represent our fears and possible tribulations. It relates on a deeper level to our emotional self.

Hearts corresponds to the element of Water,
and represent the astrological signs
Cancer, Scorpio and Pisces.

Water is viewed as being both beautiful and dangerous at the same time. Think of the ocean and all its' splendor, and yet is has the ability to create chaos. If Hearts dominate the spread, then the reading is related to emotional and personal matters of the heart, and relationships.

Clubs

Key word or phrase:
Personal Talents, Goals & Ambitions

Clubs speak to goals, dreams and ambitions. It may symbolize both conflict and resolution. It is the power of our thoughts and words, representing our secret dreams and ideas. Clubs deal with our passions. The ambition of Clubs is not financial, but based on recognition, the need to be saluted for our efforts.

Clubs corresponds to the element of Fire,
and represent the astrological signs
Aries, Leo and Sagittarius.

Fire is exceptionally beautiful and has the ability to entrance us, but one must be careful not to get to close as fire can also can burn and destroy. When Clubs dominate a spread of cards, the reading is related to deep desire, success and recognition, but also holds our secrets.

Elizabeth Melo, MHs. M

Diamonds

Key word or phrase:
Finance, Career & Possession

Diamonds are related to financial and practical areas of life, and things we have achieved or will achieve in our life time. It represents cards of material possession, career and health related issues. Diamonds are anything physical and material, finances and property.

Diamonds corresponds to the element of Earth, and represent the astrological signs Taurus, Virgo and Capricorn.

Earth is creative passion, it feeds the spirit, and nourishes. Yet, Earth can be cold and harsh if we become buried in its depths and forget to bask in the sunlight. When Diamonds are in the majority, it indicates matters related to finances or material things, as well as the physical view of life.

Spades

Key word or phrase:
Intellect, Trials & Challenges

Spades are the deeper root or core of our mind. It holds a double edge sword and represents two sides of the coin, or duality. It can represent hurt, worry or deception, but can also lead to greatness and achievement through understanding. It rules impulsive behavior and hard decisions. Spades hold strong messages, but either way, it faces the dark night of the soul, that will also lead us to ultimate victory.

Spades corresponds to the element of Air,
and represent the astrological signs
Gemini, Libra and Aquarius.

Air is the mystery that bestows unknown forces that can disrupt existence. It can be the tornado of a lifetime, yet be the calm in the eye of the storm, and gives breath to our spirit. When Spades are the dominating force in a reading, it indicates behavior, mental health, mental attitude and state of mind.

Ace's – "A" (also 1)

Key word or phrase:
New beginnings and Adventure
A time for Risk

Aces (A) represents raw energy coming into form. Seeing two or more Ace's in a spread is exciting and denotes a time of merriment! In indicates there is change on the horizon and the spark of new adventures are at hand. Aces indicate a time for boldness, chances, and taking risks with an invigorating approach.

Aces indicate new beginnings and embarking new adventures.

Fear not your boldness

This is usually a positive sign, and that the potential is there to manifest our desires in all aspects of our life. The surrounding cards will indicate more closely what the new beginnings relate to. The dominating suit will tell you more.

What we can conclude is that the seeker has weathered the storm and the initial changes, no matter how sublime, are at hand and should be met with enthusiasm that will bring us closer to fulfilling our dreams.

Bear in mind that beginnings also indicate endings and that in order for there to be beginnings something else has ended or will end. Reaching a conclusion to a part of our lives is never easy, the warning here is to let go of the past, and move forward with grace and be open to experience. Two Ace's that are side by side (close proximity) always represents a reunion, or something from the past is resurfacing.

Two's – "2"

Key word or phrase:
Holding on to Faith & Balance,
Two of Kind and Duality

Two's represent duality, much like the expression, two hearts that beat as one. But it can indicate a partnership of any kind including family, friends and business. It also serves to remind the seeker to hold on to their faith, don't give up, and maintain balance in their life.

Two's serve to remind us to keep our faith,
don't stop believing in magic
and the power of our mind.

A time to find balance within

Two's follow closely to Aces, meaning that new things have already arrived. Believe in yourself and the presence of instinct while direction is taking form. It symbolizes that you are on the right track.

Although this is very encouraging, it also indicates that the seeker might take their good fortune for granted. It's easy to slip into complacency and sway from the predominant path.

Also important to remember is that duality can be tricky, and that it can also indicate that there are two faces, and makes the truth harder to understand. The seeker should maintain integrity and minimally watch for hidden agendas.

Three's – "*3*"

Key word or phrase:
Change & Choice
Rivalry or Competition

Three's signify changes and choices presenting in the near future. When two or more three's are present in a reading, it indicates that there is more involved in the situation than what meets the eye. The most important message of seeing Three's is that change is coming and the right attitude is required.

Completion or Complication.
That is the question! What is the secret?

Stand at attention, be present in the moment

Symbolic of the three points of the triangle, when three's are predominate, there is a strong indication that choices are on the table. These choices depend on the strongest suit, for example, hearts is choices in love, clubs are choices in career, diamonds is the choice in investments and money, and spades is the choice in the mental direction of our lives, may even indicate infidelity, as in more than two in a love triangle.

Three's can indicate secrets being kept, and a clandestine air around the seeker. Either the Seeker is keeping secrets and will need to be careful of being caught in a lie or secrets are being kept by another that effects the seeker. Either way the truth will be revealed. Three's can also showcase insecurities, and a need to rediscover ourselves.

Four's – "*4*"

Key word or phrase:
Hard work & Maintain Control to build upon a Masterpiece

Four's direct us towards sustaining our actions, and maintaining structure in our lives. It reveals that a solid foundation has been laid, and that action is required to build upon the momentum. If left alone, it can slip away, but if realized in can lead to a masterpiece.

*Everything you need is available,
but it requires action and work
to see things through to completion.*

Do not stand still too long and miss opportunities

Fours focus primarily on practical matters. It denotes that there is a need to work hard, in order to achieve our hearts desire. It may not come easy but it will be worth the effort. Staying motivated is the key to accomplishment.

The warning of the four's is a refusal to change patterns or the inability to commit. Help is available if it is sought out. It warns the seeker to turn a watchful eye to personal matters.

Fives's – "5"

Key word or phrase:
Rapid change & Attention to Details
Prepare for Swift Action

Five's is fixated on the mind and soul, and advises a need to replenish the self. Rapid change is coming and preparation is required. The unknown force is like a world wind, get ready for radical changes.

Brace yourself for change,
creation is at work when Five's are present.
Expect the unexpected.

Forewarned is forearmed!

Five's remind the seeker to pay attention to their surroundings. Messages and signs are everywhere. It indicates that both the question and the answer are nearby, but there is still much instability surrounding the reading, and suggests that the seeker is having difficulty seeing the big picture clearly.

The seeker may feel a sense of loss or a need for freedom, feeling trapped in a unpredictable cycle and it will be important to prepare for these changes.

Six's – "*6*"

Key word or phrase:
Victory after Struggle,
Conflict along the Path

Six's are stating that there is a need to let go of past, and finally move forward. There are solutions available, but action is required. New found balance is within reach but requires a strong focus and avoidance of negativity. Only then can harmony come.

> *There can be eventual victory and clarity,*
> *but much struggle along the way.*
> *It's up to you!*
>
> *Gather your strength*

Here the seeker is encouraged to remain uncompromised on their integrity in order to maintain stability and positive energy. By surrounding ourselves with friends and family, we can overcome our struggle and find eventual victory.

The most important message for Six's is to find ways to stay motivated. A positive state of mind will bring a sense of hope, when someone is feeling a state of depression, or feeling down.

Get outdoors, breath the fresh air, find the joy and beauty of simple things.

Seven's – "*7*"

Key word or phrase:
Opportunity Presents,
and Luck is on Your Side
Delight in the Present Moment

Seven's is action and luck. It is the number for miracles, facing the facts of circumstances and the options that are indicated, to making changes accordingly. This is the time to build upon your dreams, make that wish board, buy that lotto ticket, and be brave and daring.

A time of new opportunities and excitement
The lucky star shines brightly upon you.

Be Brave and Daring!!!

Seven's are everywhere we look. There are the 7 wonders, the 7 colors of the rainbow, 7 days of the week, 7 continents, 7 days of creation, and so on.

This is a good time for the seeker to find their strength during the time of Seven's so that they can overcome fear of the unknown, embrace a fresh start and push forward past the doubt. They will be rewarded for their bravery.

Elizabeth Melo, MHs. M

Eight's – "8"

Key word or phrase:
A change in luck, good or bad
Forces of Nature are Strong.

Eights indicate change is coming, and it may be good or it may be bad, only the supporting cards can indicate if this is a warning or a time to embrace. Either way Eights are about change, and preparation and require attention.

The force of nature is both impressive and terrifying.
Learn to embrace the storm, for nature can be unforgiving.

In every storm there is always beauty

Eights are also indicative of new beginnings, but in the most extreme sense. Eights remind us to remain determined and responsible for our actions, that when we embrace the storm, we will find the calm.

Although likely the Eight's are more representative of good luck, then bad, there is change ahead, and the forces of nature cannot be ignored, in order to avert disaster. Hold on tight and get ready for change, when the storms come you can wash away your fears and embrace the transformation.

Nine's – "*9*"

Key word or phrase:
Growth, Communication,
Enlightenment

Nine's just might be the number you were waiting for. Nine's bring us a sense of living a dreaming. There are conclusions at hand and open communication. There is a feeling of bliss, and contentment and happiness are present.

*Coming full circle and reaching a state of bliss,
enlightenment brings harmony*

Wisdom is the capital of our journey

This indicates that the seeker has worked to find a place in their life where everything seems to be going well, and contentment is present. The seeker has lived to achieve their goals, and have become wise and responsible.

Either way, Nine's express the feeling of contentment that is either present or nearby. When this number arrives in your cards you can relax, as you are on the right path, whether you know it or not. Nine's indicates that the seeker is in a good place in life and feeling at peace with the direction of their life.

Elizabeth Melo, MHs. M

Ten's – "*10*"

Key word or phrase:
Endings or Completion,
Contentment

Ten's point to completed projects or reaching the end of the line, and is usually followed by a feeling of contentment. This can be related to career, relationships and practical issues. Ten's symbolize goals have been reached and a phase of happiness and contentment can be expected.

Take from the past all that is good
and bringing it into the future

Discard the rest, you don't need it

While this ends a cycle in life, it also marks the beginning of new adventures. Therefore representing rebirth Ten's break down to One's, the Ace's which also signifies new beginnings. Ten's tell us that we have learned a lot from the past and are ready to move into the great unknown.

It is important to realize here that endings can be difficult for the seeker. But with Ten's hope is the theme of the reading, but the dawn of a new day can bring us new dreams and direction.

Jack's – "J"

Key word or phrase:
Communication, Movement
News is on the way

Jack's can be read in different ways in a spread of cards, however when two or more Jack's are present, it suggests travel, forward movement, a time of action. It also suggests that news is one the way. Pay attention to the surrounding cards in order to more closely decipher the meaning of repeated Jack's.

Forward movement, and a time of travel
News you are waiting for is on the way

Don't be frightened by change, embrace it

Jack's also portray a younger person or immature attitudes. Jack's can also be read from an astrological point of view, which indicates personality traits as indicated by the suit.

Next to a King or Queen, it can indicate age, or maturity level. Next to fertility it may indicate children or birth of a child. Alone it may describe younger people in our lives.

The individual Jack's by suit will provide more information on what they mean.

Queen's – "Q"

Key word or phrase:
Femininity & Competition
Celebration or Gossip

Queen's symbolize women and femininity. When two or more Queen's are present in a reading it indicates competition, attending large events, such as a wedding, or party.

A sense of competition is close at hand.
Don't participate in Gossip
or be cautious of being the target of gossip

Celebrate your achievements, and the achievements of others.

It also warns the seeker of too much talking, and suggests that the seeker not participate in gossip, and to watch what they are saying. Hold secrets, and don't participate.

Queen's also portray the physical traits of the woman present in a spread, or her astrological element, the different facets to a personality. The individual Queen's will provide you with more information on personality.

Queen's also can indicate physical appearance, primarily hair color, also related to the individual card.

King's – "*K*"

Key word or phrase:
Masculinity & Authority
Important Decisions

King's symbolize men and masculinity. When two or more King's are present meetings by authority (this does not necessarily mean men, and can also represent women in authority), and important decisions are being made.

Three or more King's symbolizes important meetings,
significant gatherings are taking place
and important decisions being made by authority.

Become the authority of you own life

King's also portray the physical traits of the man present in a spread, or his astrological element, the different facets to a personality. The individual King will provide you with more information on his personality.

King's also represent physical appearance, primarily hair color, also related to the individual card.

Joker's – "J"

Key word or phrase:
Upheaval and Passion, Change or Confusion
Roller Coaster Ride

The Joker represents a lightning bolt striking the cards to their very core. It is a time of upheaval and symbolizes unpredictable zig zags of emotions and circumstances, good or bad.

The Joker is passion by storm.
The seeker is on a Roller Coaster and
should expect the unexpected.

I would rather have passion in a storm
then to live each day in an empty vessel

Joker's are a strong indication of radical behavior and sudden changes. Whether the changes are good or bad can only be determined by the surrounding cards that will help interpret the upcoming events. Either way it is a time of confusion and emotional upheaval.

The Meaning of Each Card

Learning Cartomancy is a true expression of divination and the closest to gypsy fortune telling. Here you will learn the meaning of the singular cards, and the key words and phrases that are available to serve as a reminder of each cards full meaning.

Example readings will be provided that will demonstrate the correlation of cards with each other. In time, and with much practice, it will become natural to consult the cards and understand the flow from card to card.

How to interpret the meaning of an individual card
and provide more detail and direction,
is to always consider the surrounding cards.

The following pages will provide detailed descriptions of each of the 52 cards found in the plain deck of cards, plus the two Jokers, which has already been described.

When asking a question,
some cards will be a definite YES,
while others are a definite NO,
and sometimes it is unclear, and the answer is a MAYBE,
a MAYBE suggests the answer depends on YOU.

A true expression of a reading will only be revealed with the combination of all the card sequences and their position in a spread.

Each card highlights a word or phrase for quick reference.

Elizabeth Melo, MHs. M

Sometimes when things appear absolute then it is vital to remember that the choice always lies with the seeker. Remember that our *Free Will*, is always first and foremost.

However, it is equally as important for the seeker to realize that they cannot change the actions of another, and only control how they react to the events and circumstances of others.

The consequences of our actions, or how we react, does not control the actions or reactions of another.

Another essential point is that the cards can indicate all of our opportunities and provide guidance, but it does take action on the seekers part to bring the events to fruition. You cannot expect to meet prince/princess charming, if you always stay at home, they won't be knocking on your door. The career opportunity you are hoping for won't simply manifest in thin air, unless you apply. You cannot take advantage of opportunities if you don't open your eyes to find them.

It takes the effort of the seeker to realize their dreams, to live with intention and embrace the magnificence only they can find. I believe there is an expression that says "you can drag the horse to water, but you cannot force it to drink", I believe John Heywood first claimed these words.

In other words, the seeker is being presented with opportunities but only in their own free will can they take advantage and manifest its true potential.

The one thing I know for sure is that the cards never ever lie. The reader may misinterpret, misunderstand or misconstrue the cards, but the cards themselves never lie.

Be inspired by the mystery and magic of the cards. Look for your truth and the answers will always be given.

Ace (A) of Hearts

Key word or phrase:
Hearts Desire, New beginnings in Love
Represents A Wish

The Ace of Hearts is symbolic of new love or renewed love. It represents feeling emotionally strong. There is much joy, love and happiness with the Ace of Hearts. If the seeker is already in a relationship, it indicates love being fortified on some level. This card also indicates that your wishes will soon materialize, however, unlike the 9 of Hearts, it does not just present itself to the seeker, some effort is required to manifest its potential.

The Ace of Hearts is always a YES!
Prepare for love.

The Ace of Hearts is also known as the secondary wish card, and reaching our Hearts Desire. It indicates that wishes are close by, but suggests time and energy must be put into goals. This card serves to enhance the message that everything is in the palm of our hand, and our effort can go a long way.

Elizabeth Melo, MHs. M

Two (2) of Hearts

Key word or phrase:
Two Hearts Beat as One

The Two of Hearts demonstrates that relationships around us are moving forward in the direction we desire. It is the symbol of partnership, whether romantic or otherwise, the relationship is one that is strong. This card indicates that a full commitment is ready to be made, and true love is present. It's the card of promise and faithfulness.

Two of Hearts is always a YES.
Prepare for important relationships, and commitment.

The two of hearts authenticates our relationships, whether they are romantic, plutonic or business, and characterizes devotion and trust. The nature of the relationship will be clearer with the surrounding cards, but either way it is a happy partnership and one the seeker can depend on.

Three (3) of Hearts

Key word or phrase:
Proposals and Propositions
The Happy Ending

The Three of Hearts is the catalyst for taking steps towards a full commitment, often indicating a marriage proposal and a time of celebration. The relationship has moved beyond the first stages of promise and is taking on a new level. However, promise and love comes in various forms, and can also represent bonds of family and friends are strong and true. Either way relationships progress in an optimal and satisfying way. Happy endings are represented.

The Three of Hearts is always a YES.
Open you heart, invest in your future, Victory is yours.

Be open to abundance and joy and the result will last a life time. This card may also indicate an invitation to a wedding or other form of celebration and commitment.

Four (4) of Hearts

Key word or phrase:
Feeling Gloomy, and Discontent
Seek out what brings you Cheerfulness

The Four of Hearts tells us that the mood right now is despondent, or dejected. It's a dismal card, not necessarily one of any long lasting effect, however, it does indicate a 'being in a rut'. This could arise from a recent disappointment, feeling downhearted, or minimally it can indicate boredom with one's life.

The Four of Hearts is unclear. MAYBE is your answer.
Place yourself in check, how your react can change everything.
Don't miss opportunities!

The Four of Hearts also brings news, but it is unclear if the news is positive or negative, and only the surrounding cards can indicate. Be careful to not be buried by your gloominess, life can change quickly when the Four of Hearts arrives.

Five (5) of Hearts

Key word or phrase:
The Soul is Searching,
Don't Think so Much And Forget to Live

Five of Hearts translates to a time of deep thought and soul searching. The dark night of the soul has passed, and yet you are bound to a feeling of loss. This is a time for introspection, a time to be still and listen to our intuition. The Five of Hearts carries the weight of the world on your shoulders, and one must give time to reflect on past decisions, and ponder the next step in life.

The Five of Hearts is always a NO.
Stagnant waters run deep, reflecting who we are,
and who we can be. Let the Spirit heal.

With the Five of Cubs there is a warning that the seeker is holding on to regrets, and it will be wise to encourage to reflect on the past, take the lessons and move on to the future, so that new opportunities are not missed.

Six (6) of Hearts

Key word or phrase:
Bonds are Strong
The Foundation of our Future

The Six of Hearts embodies all our relationships, including marriage, family, friendship and career. It is the solidification of your bonds that form the foundation of life. These bonds are not easily broken, and the Six of Hearts is a sign of life time commitments. It also leans towards revisiting the past, or perhaps encountering someone from the past reappearing, an old friend or lover. But know that if this is the case, you will be at your very best, and feeling on top of the world.

The Six of Hearts is always a YES.
Say hello to the past
so that you can lay the foundation of your future.

By reconciling our past, we can leave it behind and look to the future with optimism and faith. Six of Hearts means a Blast from the past.

Seven (7) of Hearts

Key word or phrase:
The Seven Best Wishes of Love
Dreams and Inspiration

Seven of Hearts epitomizes romantic gestures often called the "seven best wishes of love". New horizons are at hand and new opportunities are highlighted. This card represents our dream realm and hidden desires. It is a reflection of a much deeper part of the seeker, and one they do not share easily. This card marks a new light is shining bright and we are embarking on a new adventure.

The Seven of Hearts is always a YES.
Look deep within to realize your dreams, hopes and desires.

The Seven of Hearts also indicates that a new light might be shining on an old situation. This is a time to look deep within to dissipate fear and confusion, and understand the true motivations so that you can chase your dreams and realize your true purpose in life. This is the time to be honest with your true self.

Eight (8) of Hearts

Key word or phrase:
Feeling unfulfilled and abandoned
Time to let go of what holds you back

The Eight of Hearts serves to remind you to move on with courage and determination. This may be a time of moving past relationships that hinder your spirit, or even moving past your own beliefs and traditions. Happiness is at hand but it comes with the cost of letting go. Sometimes is changing in your life or changing in your lifestyle brought on my health or finances.

The Eight of Hearts is unclear. MAYBE is your answer.
Letting go can lead to celebration and success.

Eight of Hearts can also denote a time of gatherings, most often in celebration with family and friends. But it requires taking the first step. It can imply attendance of significant social events, and a great deal of activities taking place.

Nine (9) of Hearts

Key word or phrase:
The Ultimate Wish Card
The future is bright

Nine of Hearts is the ultimate Wish card and brings us reward, joy, happiness and bliss. In embodies the ecstasy of pleasure and harmony and tells us that the future is overflowing with all that is cherished and is a powerful omen that you will be truly happy. The Nine of Hearts is a time of peace and fulfillment.

The Nine of Hearts is always a YES, YES, YES.
The cup overflows with abundance.

How our wishes unravel depends upon the surrounding cards. The cards surrounding the Nine of Hearts may hint at any challenges that we may meet, or can suggest that what we wish for may not be what is right for us, often following the expression "Be careful what you wish for, you just might get it".

Ten (10) of Hearts

Key word or phrase:
Pleasant Surprises and Exciting Times
Fulfilment and Contentment

The Ten of Hearts is best known as the buffer card, it automatically negates and cancels negative energy or any negative cards that might surround it. It provides you with protection no matter how bleak things may appear at present. The Ten of Hearts also symbolizes big surprises, and suggests exciting times ahead. Nothing can really spoil the moment when this card is present.

The Ten of Hearts is always a YES.
There is no mountain you cannot climb, and
no bridge you cannot cross.

When the Ten of Hearts appears your goals are realized, all your turmoil will be resolved, your dreams will come true, you are on solid ground, and the moment is unshakeable.

Ace (A) of Clubs

Key word or phrase:
Gifts, Achievements, Rewards
Distinctive Talent and Curious Mind

Ace of Clubs is elite recognition, a special achievement, receiving an award or being known for a distinctive talent that will lead to reward. It is also the implication of a gift however this gift may come in more than one way, such as in the case of a material gift, gift of foresight, or the gift of love.

The Ace of Clubs is always a YES.
Greatness is your gift, capitalize on the moment,
allow yourself to be transformed.

The Ace of Clubs indicates that your true destiny is great success, let the creativity flow through you, take a chance and allow yourself to be inspired.

Elizabeth Melo, MHs. M

Two (2) of Clubs

Key word or phrase:
Communication, Focus,
Laying the Ground Work towards Goals

Two of Clubs represents the start of a new venture, requiring a clear focus. This could also indicate a partnership that is beneficial to realizing true success. The Two of Clubs foreshadows communication, a direct interchange between two sources, personal or professional.

The Ace of Clubs is unclear, MAYBE is your answer.
Stay focused and be prepared to reap your rewards.

Staying focused during the time of the Ace of Clubs will be important, as there is a clear indication that the seeker may become overwhelmed, and feel insecure.

Three (3) of Clubs

Key word or phrase:
The Choice Presents to flourish:
Move forward or Remain Stuck

With the Three of Clubs the time has come to walk away from the past, or the present circumstances are coming to an end. You may choose to sever ties with a lover, friend or perhaps walking away from a job. Either way as the word severing implies it is a completion, with no strings remaining. The choice is presented.

The Ace of Clubs is always NO.
Sever the ties that bind you to unhappiness.
Open yourself to new experiences to reach your potential.

If you choose to walk away your creativity and inventiveness will abound. New Career opportunities may arise, it's a time to take chances. Allow yourself to be challenged mentally and intellectually.

Four (4) of Clubs

Key word or phrase:
Moving, Security, Balance
Time to Rest and Replenish

With the Four of Clubs comes a time to rest and recharge. Security, balance and initial success are achieved. Peace has been found, and rest and recharging is required before taking on the challenges that lay in the horizon. However, one should not stay to long in this position, as change will come at any moment.

The Four of Clubs is unclear, and MAYBE is your answer.
Rest and replenish but only for a moment.
Don't risk missing out on what comes next.

Soon after the Four of Clubs appears in a reading, it advises the seeker that there will soon be movement of some kind, this could be a residential move, taking a holiday, moving to a new job or position within a workplace, or simply moving away from conflict.

Five (5) of Clubs

Key word or phrase:
Masks to be revealed, Secrets to be Unveiled
Maintaining Balance during Struggle

The Five of Clubs reveals that there are secrets and the preverbal mask is falling and the truth will be unveiled. It can imply that a person close to the seeker is not showing their true colors, and that what you see is not necessarily what you get. It implies deceit at a profound level. But know that the truth will surface when this card is present.

The Five of Clubs is always a NO.
What you see, may not be what you get.
Open your eyes and observe.

The Five of Clubs suggests a time of struggle, and advises us to pay attention, and be careful of miscommunication, avoid quarrels, and trust in your instincts to know where the truth lies.

Six (6) of Clubs

Key word or phrase:
Sexuality, Intimacy, Understanding
Approach life with Grace and Diplomacy

The Six of Clubs guides us towards embracing our successes with grace, and warns to not over indulge or become overbearing. Overconfidence leads to vanity and arrogance.

The Six of Clubs is unclear, MAYBE is your answer.
Welcome new opportunities with grace and diplomacy.

The Six of Clubs symbolizes personal sexuality and intimate encounters. The essence of the card must be determined by its surrounding cards. It can indicate sexual satisfaction or questions regarding sexuality, or perhaps the seeker is going to experience a new dynamic in an intimate relationship. It is important to approach the subject of sexuality carefully regardless of its positive or negative connotation. Take great care to understand its meaning through the surrounding cards.

Seven (7) of Clubs

Key word or phrase:
The Unforeseen, Obstacles
Persist with Dedication to Succeed

The Seven of Clubs brings about the unforeseen and that we are feeling distant and unfocused. Sometimes it can indicate that we cannot see what is directly before us, or as the expression says, 'you cannot see the forest for the trees'. There is a strong indication that the seeker is feeling of weary and disillusioned.

The Seven of Clubs always a NO.
Time to let go of doubt and persevere in the
face of challenge and overcome our fear.

This is the time to dig into your reserve and find your endurance through the unknown territory. Conflicts will arise, and only looking within yourself will you find the strength to rise above and overcome obstacles. Although this card comes shrouded with warning, it also encourages us to find our strengths and persist.

Eight (8) of Clubs

Key word or phrase:
Gambler's Card, Luck, Eventful
A Time of Reward through Diligence

Eight of Clubs is the card of luck, often referred to as the 'gamblers lucky card'. This is a time to plant your feet firmly on the ground, as the tendency can be to over indulge. Instead, embrace the moment, and remain diligent.

The Eight of Clubs always a YES.
On Your Mark! Get Ready! AND GO!

This is a time when things will happen quickly, and expect to be moving at a fast pace, so buckle your seat belt, take chances but play it safe. Bear in mind that a change of luck can happen at any moment, but that luck by its very essence implies sudden change whether coincidence or synchronicity, but either way it comes as a phase in life and not an isolated moment.

Nine of Clubs

Key word or phrase:
Overall Wealth
Wealth of the Heart, Soul and Material

A card to love! The Nine of Clubs is an excellent omen that says the seeker is reaching their destination, full potential and fulfillment in life. Overall wealth is at hand, meaning wealth of the heart, mind and spirit, along with financial security. It is reaching a phase of ultimate happiness.

The Nine of Clubs always a YES.
Coming full circle, it is time to embrace happiness and success.

The Nine of Clubs tell us that you have come a long way through your courage and commitment, now it is time to rest and enjoy all the riches you have been rewarded. You are a Rock Star! You have made it through many struggles and now you can expect a long while of contentment with no worries.

Ten (10) of Clubs

Key word or phrase:
Unexpected Sum of Money,
Financial Increase, Achievements

The Ten of Clubs resembles opening a new door in life, or beginning a new chapter. It is a time to celebrate achievements and the completion of a cycle in life, and yet find reminds to appreciation in all that you have. This card can imply and inheritance or receiving a lump sum of money through winnings, regarding financial increase is emanate.

The Ten of Clubs is always a YES.
Good fortune befalls, and the time has come to pamper
the inner spirit, so that we may appreciate our prosperity.

Remaining humble is the key, as this card has come to you after a time of hardship. You have earned this time in your life, and here you will find peace of mind, financial security, spiritual fulfillment, and a heart filled with love. Enjoy you good fortune.

Ace (A) of Diamonds

Key word or phrase:
A Gift, Reward, Stability
Material Gains through Efforts

The Ace of Diamonds is a positive card, bringing with it new beginnings as with all the Aces. This is a time when projects fall into place, ideas are forming, and you are willing and ready to take it on. Hard work will lead to material gains. Little things will bring you joy and energy to forge forward with your dreams.

The Ace of Diamonds is always a YES.
A simple gesture of flowers can say so much.
A time for prosperity and success.

If you have an idea, then move forward, the future looks bright. This card also implies receiving a gift, or promise that will be sentimental. This can be small like flowers from a lover, or something more significant such as a ring, or potential engagement. The supporting cards will give you more.

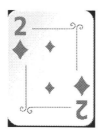

Two (2) of Diamonds

Key word or phrase:
Balance is key, Prudence
Be mindful of finances,

Two of Diamonds is not a critical card on financial concerns however it does indicate that an unexpected expense has or will occur shortly. This can be problems with a vehicle, or a home improvement project costing a little more than expected. Its basic meaning suggests that money is being spent on something that was not expected.

The Two of Diamonds is a definite NO.
Surprise opportunities might cost you.
Listen to your instincts and be cautious in spending money

Financially, there could be some ups and downs when the Two of Diamonds is present, likely on the financial front. There is a strong indication of challenges ahead, but nothing life shattering; however laying out a back-up plan is the best option.

Three (3) of Diamonds

Key word or phrase:
Accomplishments, Investments
Success through Personal Effort

Three of Diamonds means something new, such as the purchase of a new home or vehicle, but usually it is be something substantial. It can be an investment of money into a new project. Hard work and mastery are compensated.

The Three of Diamonds is a definite YES.
It might be time for a new home or a new project!
Either way resources are available, let the process begin.

This time in the seekers life is not brought on by sheer luck, but rather by cleverness, dedication, and tenacity. This is a well-deserved small victory. The advice given by the Three of Diamonds is maintaining the status quo but keep moving along this path with caution. Trust in the rewards that will come and revel in the small victories along the way.

Elizabeth Melo, MHs. M

Four (4) of Diamonds

Key word or phrase:
Overly Cautious, Indecision
Paralyzed by Fear divorced from Reality

The Four of Diamonds, when it stands alone indicates a time of indecisions. Its truer meaning is revealed by the surrounding cards, as indecision can be in any part of life, whether romantic insecurity, financial spending, and any indecision related to our life. It symbolizes having trouble reconciling our feelings.

The Four of Diamonds is unclear, MAYBE is your answer.
Don't become paralyzed by fear so much that
you miss out on life's adventures.

The Found Diamonds indicates that the seeker is consumed by fear that is divorced from reality and therefore unable to see the situation clearly. The seeker should be encouraged to move past their fear, as it is not founded in this case.

Five (5) of Diamonds

Key word or phrase:
Journey, Frontward or Backwards
Choosing Direction

The Five of Diamonds indicates an upcoming journey. This journey may be short or long depending on the surrounding cards, and it can be either personal or professional, but a trip is definitely on the horizon. This trip can be either by land or via air travel. The nature of the trip will be clear made clear.

The Five of Diamonds is a definite Yes.
You choose, will your Journey take your forward,
or will you move backwards.

The time of the Five of Diamonds is movement, but do we move forward in the direction of our goals and set our priorities for success, or do we move backwards and continue to repeat the same story. Learn the lesson and move on is the theme.

Six (6) of Diamonds

Key word or phrase:
Fertility, Growth, Birth, Pay it forward
Generosity will be rewarded

The Six of Diamonds symbolizes fertility and birth. However fertility can come in many forms. It may indicate a birth of a child or news of a pregnancy, but it may also imply a birth of a new relationship or professional growth. It signifies that there are increases such as growing investments or the symbolic rebirth of the soul. This card is followed with brightness and happiness.

The Six of Diamonds is a definite Yes.
Your bigheartedness will bring you the kindness you deserve.

The Six of Diamonds can also convey that your success is due to your generosity, or a generosity bestowed of another bestowed upon you. With the Six of Diamonds investments are paying off, finances are increasing, the sharing of rewards and paying it forward in kindness.

Seven (7) of Diamonds

Key word or phrase:
Expect Delays, Patience
Retreat to Fight another Day

The Seven of Diamonds alludes to a time that things are not progressing as hoped, and warns of unforeseen delays. However delays can be viewed as a necessary time to ponder what is best, what your next move should be and that 'good things come to those who wait'. It advises to wait it out, be patient, that all will come in due course.

The Seven of Diamonds is a definite NO.
Take no immediate action for the time being,
ponder the situation before proceeding and don't lose hope.

The Seven of Diamonds is a time to trust in the process, and understand that slow and steady wins the race. Success is eventual with this card, but it is best to not take any chances or risks for the moment, and trust that things will play out in your favour.

Elizabeth Melo, MHs. M

Eight (8) of Diamonds

Key word or phrase:
Health, Possible Financial Loss
A Time for Nourishing the Soul

As with most cards, the Eight of Diamonds true meaning is revealed by its surrounding cards. Generally, it regards our health, and can be a warning to have a medical check-up that could prevent bigger problems. However, it may indicate a financial loss, so this is a time for being cautious.

The Eight of Diamonds is a definite NO.
It's time to rest... listen to your inner self.
It's time to nourish your body, mind & spirit

With the Eight of Diamonds, it may also imply that times are tight with finances and caution should be exercised in spending money to prevent further stress. Sometimes this loss can be related to divorce or custody. It can also indicate that someone is working in medicine or related field.

Nine (9) of Diamonds

Key word or phrase:
Advancement, Promises of Success
Promotions and Security

The Nine of Diamonds is a change in career or job, or advancement of some sort, such as a promotion. It is definitely symbolic of a new venture in life, and may even suggest advancing education or retraining. This new venture should be perceived as a good stepping stone. However, depending on the cards around it, it can indicate meeting a person of significance, or an authority figure.

The Nine of Diamonds is a definite YES.
Make plans, take action.
Take the steps required to instigate positive change.

The Nine of Diamonds can also suggest wishes on a more monetary level, such as wishing for a promotion, or new job. It's a positive card from a more masculine perspective. This is a time to make plans and take action, and watch rewards roll in on the tides. This is a time for happiness and contentment.

Ten (10) of Diamonds

Key word or phrase:
Completion, Success, Buried Treasure
Fated for Greatness

The seeker has reached a pivotal moment in their life when the Ten of Diamonds arrives, suggesting that with finances and successes have been attained and there is a feeling of completeness. This card can also imply a sudden wind-fall of money, such as a raise in earnings through employment or investments. Either way, money matters are boding well. This card may even advise that now is a good time to invest in new projects or ideas.

The Ten of Diamonds is a definite YES.
Make plans, take action.
Take the steps required to instigate positive change.

The Ten of Diamonds offers stability, prosperity and a time for enjoyment. Your financial security and emotional well-being are both positively indicated by the presence of this card in your spread. You may just find your hidden treasure

Ace (A) of Spades

Key word or phrase:
The End, Death, Transformation
Loss and Dramatic Change

The Ace of Spades indicates that a significant ending is coming, and a dramatic change can be expected. As with all aces, new beginnings are represented, however we must experience a time of morning and sadness. Known as the death card, it symbolizes any significant ending, such as ending a relationship, a divorce, or physical transition into another world.

The Ace of Spades is a definite NO.
Allow the hurt and pain, so that you may shed the past.
Time to Wait out the storm, and the calm will follow.

Change with the Ace of Spades will be major, a dramatic. It will always follow with some pain, hurt and a sense of loss. It can represent cutting the ties between our past and our present, so that the future will not be bound to tradition, and the slate is wiped clean.

Two (2) of Spades

Key word or phrase:
Stalemate, Vigilance, Deceit, Lies,
Opposing Forces Block Our Path

The Two of Spades is the card of deception. Although it can imply the seeker is keeping secrets, or that secrets are being kept from the seeker, it generally counsels that secrets will create conflict. Vigilance is required, as the truth is known to prevail in the end. Not is the time to listen to your instincts. Trust yourself.

The Two of Spades is unclear, MAYBE is your answer.
Place yourself in check, prepare for the struggles ahead.
Only resolution will bring you peace on your journey.
The path will clear eventually.

The Two of Spades represents the cross-roads, and no clear path is available for the moment, you are in a stalemate position and in a time of confusion. Expect to be blindsided by hidden forces. Remain still for a moment until it passes.

Three (3) of Spades

Key word or phrase:
Choice, Separation, Duplicity
Betrayal and Emotional Loss

Three of Spades conveys a story that outside influences are interfering in the seekers life. It indicates betrayal, whether on a personal level or professionally and it can only be determined by the surrounding cards. Either way this card means there are hidden influences at work. Ultimately it will lead to choices and decisions. The status quo will erupt. This card suggests that 'three is a crowd', and that a difficult time can be anticipated.

The Three of Spades is a definite NO.
Pain will lead to new beginnings, but you must face the truth.
A time for evaluation, let go to make room for change.

When the eruption happens with the Three of Spades, it will be time to evaluate the situation, redesign our priorities in the face of heartbreak. Don't allow yourself to be overcome by misery and anguish.

Four (4) of Spades

Key word or phrase:
Legal Issues, Legal Papers,
Ceasefire, Negotiate, Call a Truce

The Four of Spades indicates legal issues, legal papers or legal problems at hand. It does not necessarily mean in a negative way, it can imply legal papers regarding a new mortgage, or new contract related to career, or on a deeper level it can be a custody or divorce battle. It can also be something simple like a speeding ticket. It can only be determined by its surrounding cards.

The Four of Spades is a definite YES.
It may be time to withdraw and ceasefire.
Paying attention to detail will catch any hidden agendas.

The Four of Spades, whether it is good or bad, it does suggest that one should pay heed to any underhandedness. Call a temporary truce in order to recover or negotiate. Think things through and remain fair minded.

Five (5) of Spades

Key word or phrase:
The Dark Night of the Soul Shall Pass
Bittersweet Recovery, Transformation

The Five of Spades denotes a time of suffering, sadness, hardship, or feeling of loss. The moment is heavy and laced with fear. It foreshadows a chapter in life that takes us through the Dark Night of the Soul. Recovery will be bittersweet but will lead to greater wisdom. Conflict leads to transformation.

The Five of Spades is a definite YES.
A time of transformation, after struggle,
as the dark night of the soul passes,
shed the cocoon, and emerge the butterfly.

The Five of Spades signifies trauma, and feeling defeated. Retreat and evaluate, what are you holding on too? Don't let insecurities impede your victory and recovery. There is a bittersweet undertone to the Five of Spades.

Six (6) of Spades

Key word or phrase:
Conflict, Discord, Disappointment,
Quarrels, Stormy Waters Lie Ahead

The Six of Spades indicates that a heated discussion or argument will occur. It is advises to keep our temperance in check to avoid a disruption becoming violent in nature, or saying things that are out of turn, and ill advised. This is the time to remember that to be forewarned it to be forearmed.

The Six of Spades is unclear, MAYBE is your answer.
Don't be dishonored by the actions of others.
Ride the Stormy Waters, and embrace your endurance.

The Six of Spades warns us that we cannot change or control the actions of another, only our reaction to the circumstances. Guard against low self-esteem and engaging in the dishonor of someone else. Be vigilant, and don't allow your disappointment to get the best of the situation. The desired outcome is within your grasp, you need only reach and embrace it

Seven (7) of Spades

Key word or phrase:
Mental Clarity after Strife,
A time to Strategize, Theft or Hurdles

The Seven of Spades follows with a feeling of being let down by something or someone. This is not a strong force, but it is one of deep retrospection in order to find metal clarity and assess the state of affairs. It will not be easy to forgive past events, and there is urgent need to move from this point and abandon disappointment as it no longer matters.

The Seven of Spades is a definite YES.
This is not the time to take heart, but to use
clear logic and intellect to surpass the hurdles.

The Seven of Spades urges the need to build on strategies to overcome hurdles and not allow frustration or emotions to dictate what happens next. Don't give in to feelings of self-pity and hinder your own growth. There is also an indication of possible theft, or misplacing an object, be vigilant on personal belongs.

Eight (8) of Spades

Key word or phrase:
Turmoil, Tumultuous Times, Incarceration
Explosive Energy, State of Mind,

The Eight of Spades is not an easy card. It indicates emotional and mental anguish. It warns of irrational behavior or in some cases mental illness or mental breakdown. Here you will find a caution to avoid explosive bursts of energy leading to difficult times. This is a time to seek out a stabilizing environment.

The Eight of Spades is a definite NO.
Self-sabotage can lead to confrontation and an
unhealthy state of mind, it wise to avoid negative energy.

The Eight of Spades cautions against allowing torment and sorrow to afflict the status quo. Fear of failure can become paralyzing, bumping the obstacles can instigate a chain reaction that will bring unfortunate circumstances. It is best to accept our limitations or restrictions for the moment. Stand still and allow this time to pass.

Nine (9) of Spades

Key word or phrase:
Despair, Suffering, Gossip, Isolation, Paranoia, A Self-imposed Prison

The Nine of Spades symbolizes despair and isolation, and suggests that one should seek out counsel in order to overcome a self-imposed prison that can lead to paranoia and despair.

The Nine of Spades is a definite NO.
Don't imprison the Spirit, and seek out the wisdom of counsel.
A caged spirit, will die unless it learns to fly.

Another indication of the Nine of Spades is the presence of gossip, whether true or false, news comes indirectly and in this case not from the source but through third part manipulation. It can even mean that we are the target of gossip and betrayal. It is important to remember that nothing in this card implies that the information received is accurate or truthful. Be sure not to participate in such gossip

Ten (10) of Spades

Key word or phrase:
Overburdened, Overwhelmed, Jealousy
Trapped by Our Own Demise

The Ten of Spades indicates that you have fallen into a state of unbalanced in life, work, home, and physical self. You have been too busy in the pursuit of the material, and neglecting the physical and spiritual self. To find happiness again, balance must be attained. Feed the spirit, meditate, exercise and dedicate yourself to a healthy diet. This is the end of a cycle, choose wisely so that the next cycle will be better.

The Ten of Spades is a definite NO.
Don't limit the spirit by falling into traps.
You can change the circumstances if you choose.

The Ten of Spades also indicates jealousy, you may be the target of jealousy or you are allowing jealousy to get the best of you. If the Ten of Spades is present, it can be determined that jealousy will become an issue and best to place yourself in check.

Court Cards
Jack's, Queen's and King's

As indicated earlier, Court cards represent people, events, personality and general appearance. It can be a little tricky to correlate them in a reading, but practice will see you through.

When they are present in a reading, it can introduce the character of a person, reveal personality traits, and signal their intentions and help understand their behavior, mannerisms and motivations. There is also an Astrological reference made to the Court cards that may help.

However, it can also indicate physical qualities such as hair color, gender and age. My advice is to form a connection with the Court cards by evaluating them individually, and decide which attributes work best for you.

Looking for clues within the cards,
will solve the mystery.
Take time to riddle it out!

There are also events or circumstances associated to each Court card. The interpretation depends mostly on understand the cards, the surrounding situations, and determining which force is being represented. Listen to your intuition, and with time it will become natural.

Prepare to learn what each Jack, Queen and King mean for each suit. How they lay out in a spread will provide a clearer picture in how to decipher their meaning.

Jack (J) of Hearts

Key word or phrase:
Cupids Arrow, Fertility, Invitations
Light to Medium Haired Youth

Jack of Hearts is associated to a young emotional persona of no particular gender, who embodies the attributes of a romantic, poetic individual, who is ruled by their heart. A relationship oriented person, who loves to love. This is a charming yet melancholy sort, who can be over emotional, and temperamental.

The Jack of Hearts is a definite YES.
Astrological represents WATER Signs and the emotional
depths that encompass Pisces, Cancer and Scorpio.

The Jack of Hearts may also represent a young light to medium haired person, often referred to as dirty blond or light brown.

This Card can pertain to news of a pregnancy, or a significant invitation. It also symbolizes Cupids Arrow and love is around the corner. Perhaps the invitation is a love proposal.

Queen (Q) of Hearts

Key word or phrase:
Compassion, Intuition, Moodiness
Light to Medium Haired Woman

The Queen of Hearts personifies motherhood. She is warm and compassionate and displays a sensitive nurturing nature. She is often sought out for comfort and counsel, as she embodies fairness and kindness. However, the Queen of Hearts can also become extremely emotional and have a tendency to be moody.

The Queen of Hearts is a definite YES.
Astrological represents WATER Signs and the emotional
depths that encompass Pisces, Cancer and Scorpio.

The Queen of Hearts represents a woman with light to medium haired, often referred to as dirty blond or light brown.

This Card can also indicate fluctuating situations, and shadowed truths. Be careful to not become disheartened.

King (K) of Hearts

Key word or phrase:
Discipline, Divine Intervention
Light to Medium Haired Man

The King of Hearts is the proverbial hard working family man, who enjoys a quite home style life, and the embodiment of a thoughtful and caring nature. He is often intrigued by spiritual matters and enjoys helping others by providing guidance and good advice. He can be prone to moodiness and introspection.

The King of Hearts is unclear, MAYBE is your answer. Astrological represents WATER Signs and the emotional depths that encompass Pisces, Cancer and Scorpio.

The King of Hearts represents a man with light to medium hair, often referred to as dirty blond or light brown.

The King of Hearts can also represent divine intervention, hidden forces that are at work on behalf of the seeker, its best to wait before making big decisions, as the way forward will soon be clear.

Jack (J) of Clubs

Key word or phrase:
Impulsive, Spontaneous, Travel
Medium to Dark Haired Person

The Jack of Clubs represents a young person, not associated to a particular gender. It personifies spontaneity and an energetic nature with great determination to achieve their goals. Their enthusiasm for life is contagious and fun. However they focus more on what others think of them, and crave attention. They can be impatient and impulsive in their decision making.

The Jack of Clubs is always NO.
Astrological represents FIRE Signs and the
ambitious driven energy of Leo, Aries and Sagittarius.

The Jack of Clubs represents a younger person with medium to dark hair, and fair complexion.

The Jack of Clubs can also indicate travel or a sudden change in environment. Be aware, it may well come on you suddenly!

Queen (Q) of Clubs

Key word or phrase:
Passionate, Leadership, Bold Action
Medium to Dark Haired Woman

The Queen of Clubs is the more dominate female who is a master of her own destiny. She is optimistic and determined, and holds clear goals and direction. She is one to face her challenges, as she embodies courage and passion. She is capable of great leadership qualities, however, she can have a tendency to be vain, and crave to be the center of attention, lending to some insecurities.

The Queen of Clubs is unclear, MAYBE is your answer.
Astrological represents FIRE Signs and the
ambitious driven energy of Leo, Aries and Sagittarius.

The Queen of Clubs represents a woman with medium to dark hair, and fair complexion.

The Queen of Clubs may also indicate new energy entering your life, and feeling open to new experiences.

King (K) of Clubs

Key word or phrase:
Dynamic, Determined, Confidence
Medium to Dark Haired Man

The King of Spades represents a strong and confident man, who is often in a leadership role. He is dynamic, sexy and fun! He is a natural born leader, who sets his goals and will accomplish them. He can tend to be at times materialistic, a master of manipulation, and shock you with a cold and selfish side.

The King of Clubs is a definite YES.
Astrological represents FIRE Signs and the
ambitious driven energy of Leo, Aries and Sagittarius.

The King of Clubs represents a man with medium to dark hair, and fair complexion.

The King of Clubs may also signify advancement, and good advice, indicating power in action, but be cautious against recklessness.

Jack (J) of Diamonds

Key word or phrase:
Patient, Slow and Steady, Honor
Fair Haired & Fair Complexed Youth

The Jack of Diamonds represents a young person of no particular gender, who is dependable and trustworthy, rich in common sense and rooted firmly on the ground. They are patient and kind and virtuous. There is a risk for melodramatic behavior.

The Jack of Diamonds is a definite YES.
Astrological represents EARTH Signs and the practical and
grounded qualities of Taurus, Virgo and Capricorn.

The Jack of Diamonds represents a young person with fair or reddish tint of hair and freckly fair complexion.

The Jack of Diamonds indicates news coming soon, sudden unexpected calls or other form of communication, but either way a positive exchange.

Queen (Q) of Diamonds

Key word or phrase:
Practical, Reliable, Worthy
Fair Haired & Fair Complexed Woman

The Queen of Diamonds is the embodiment of a woman is who rooted in traditional values. She is dependable, trustworthy, and down to earth and sensual in nature. She tends to be practical, domestic and reliable. Slow and steady she wins the race. However, she is capable of stubborn pride and can have an unforgiving nature.

The Queen of Diamonds is a definite YES.
Astrological represents EARTH Signs and the practical and
grounded qualities of Taurus, Virgo and Capricorn.

The Queen of Diamonds represents a woman with fair or reddish tint of hair and freckly fair complexion.

The Queen of Diamonds indicates journey and achievement through hard work.

King (K) of Diamonds

Key word or phrase:
Loyal, Devoted, Stability
Fair Haired & Fair Complexed Man

The King of Diamonds represents a man who is loyal and devoted. He is often fun-loving and charming, and people are drawn to be by his side. He is a father figure, who cares deeply for others. He is dependable, caring, soft hearted and wise. He can also be lethargic and exceptionally stubborn.

The King of Diamonds is unclear, MAYBE is your answer. Astrological represents EARTH Signs and the practical and grounded qualities of Taurus, Virgo and Capricorn.

The King of Diamonds represents a man with fair or reddish tint of hair and freckly fair complexion.

The King of Diamonds denotes a time of abundance, suggesting advancement at work, promotion and increase in finances.

Jack (J) of Spades

Key word or phrase:
Spontaneous, Charming, Intellectual
Dark Haired & Rich Complexed Youth

The Jack of Spades personifies a young person who tends to be charming, impulsive and spontaneous. They are remarkably sharp, intellectual abstract thinkers, usually with a high IQ. They are the inventors, creative souls, who can sometimes be unreliable and childish

The Jack of Spades is unclear. MAYBE is your answer.
Astrological represents Air Signs and the spontaneous, intellectual
abstract thinkers of Gemini, Libra and Aquarius.

The Jack of Spades represents a youth of no particular gender with dark hair and rich complexion.

The Jack of Spades suggests a time of letting your intellectual side rule, as opposed to the heart.

Elizabeth Melo, MHs. M

Queen (Q) of Spades

Key word or phrase:
Independent, Unpredictable, Keen Minded Dark Haired & Rich Complexed Woman

The Queen of Spades personifies a charming, impulsive and independent woman, with an innate ability to understand the mind of others, and uncanny power to pluck the answers out of thin air. She is fiercely passionate in her beliefs, however, she is also unpredictable in love. She can be complicated, and at times radical in her behavior, always expect a challenge with her.

The Queen of Spades is always NO.
Astrological represents Air Signs and the spontaneous, intellectual abstract thinkers of Gemini, Libra and Aquarius.

The Queen of Spades represents a woman with dark hair and rich complexion.

The Queen of Spades represents a creative endeavor one that could lead to great success if seen through to the end.

King (K) of Spades

Key word or phrase:
Friendly, Loyal, Fair Minded
Dark Haired & Rich Complexed Man

The King of Spades is a friendly, charming man who is highly intelligent, loyal and assertive. This man tends to be a creative independent thinker, with a keen mind for fairness and balance. He is has a knack for drawing people to him with his talent of intense observation, however, he is motivated by intellect and becomes bored quickly, and is unlikely emotionally invested.

The King of Spades is always NO.
Astrological represents Air Signs and the spontaneous, intellectual
abstract thinkers of Gemini, Libra and Aquarius.

The King of Spades represents a man with dark hair and rich complexion.

The King of Spades represents a possible encounter with a man in uniform connected to the law or position of power.

Art of Cartomancy & Spreads

When learning to read cards, it is important to get as much from the different spreads as you can. The more you practice the art of Cartomancy, you will begin to build relationships between the cards, understand the patterns that are being communicated and the message being received.

Take some time to shuffle, and play with your cards. Let your energy flow through them and build a connection. You may even choose to sleep with them under your pillow to really form this connection. The connection between you and the cards is to enhance the experience however, it is not necessary when it comes to the plain deck. As long as you have your own connection to the divine self, and have truly worked on building your intuition, you can read cards anytime, anyplace and any deck.

Before you do a reading for yourself or someone else, be sure to be in a comfortable position, and take a few deep breaths to help quiet the chatter in your mind. This enforces your connection to the intuition. Shuffle the cards several times to clear away any past influence or energy from the previous readings. Concentrate on opening your mind to receiving messages.

While you are shuffling place your intention in the cards. You can do this by stating quietly in your mind "I am grateful to the Universe for providing me with guidance". Remember this is about energy, and the Universe is the greatest energy of all. Be sure to concentrate on your intent.

When you are doing a reading for someone else, you follow the same steps, and focus your intention on helping them.

Ask the Seeker to begin by shuffling the cards for as long as they desire and to focus on their questions, concerns and make a wish. The same applies if you are self-reading.

Encourage the seeker to be as specific as possible when formulating the thoughts in their mind, and when they are ready, they may cut the deck into three separate piles.

You, as the reader, should restack the cards and begin to spread the cards into the layout of your choice.

Using the Spreads is a pattern to laying out the cards, and assist in deciphering their meanings according to their position. Refer to the spreads in this book to get you started.

Once you have laid out the cards into their position, take a few moments to assess the overall essence and overtone of the reading. You can do this my reflecting on the most prominent suit (Hearts, Clubs, Diamonds and Spades) and the number sequences. First assess the predominant suit. Please read the earlier chapters on Suits and Number sequence for their full meaning

---

A Quick Recap On Suits

Hearts ♥ corresponds to the element of Water
correlates to matters of the heart
Clubs ♣ corresponds to the element of Fire
correlates to personal talents, goals and ambitions
Diamonds ♦ corresponds to the element of Earth
correlates to finance, career and material possession
Spades ♠ corresponds to the element of Air
correlates to the intellect, trials and challenges.

Elizabeth Melo, MHs. M

Once you have concluded the predominant suit, your next step is to gauge the repeating numbers, as this will further advise on the overtone of the reading.

A Quick Recap On Number Sequence	
Ace's (A) (also 1)	New beginnings and Adventure
Two's (2)	Holding on to Faith & Balance, Duality
Three's (3)	Change & Choice
Four's (4)	Hard work to build upon a Masterpiece
Fives's (5)	Rapid change & Attention to Details
Six's (6)	Victory after Struggle, Conflict
Seven's (7)	Opportunity Presents, and Lucky Omen
Eight's (8)	A change in luck, Forces of Nature
Nine's (9)	Growth, Communication, Enlightenment
Ten's (10)	Endings or Completion, Contentment
Jack's (J)	Communication, Movement, Travel
Queen's (Q)	Competition,Celebration, Gossip
King's (K)	Authority, Important Meetings
Joker's (J)	Upheaval and Passion, Change or Confusion, emotional roller coaster

Now that you have done an overview of the overall essence of the reading you are ready to begin deciphering the spreads, and correlating the readings.

A Quick Recap On Hearts ♥

The following is a quick reference Guide to the meaning of each card in the Hearts Suit. It is important to read the full meanings of each card first, and to use this as a point of reference only.

Ace (A)	Hearts Desire, New beginnings in Love, Represents Wishes	YES
Two (2)	Two Hearts Beat as One	YES
Three (3)	Proposals and Propositions The Happy Ending	YES
Four (4)	Gloomy, and Discontent, Seek out what brings you Cheerfulness	MAYBE
Five (5)	The Soul is Searching, Don't think so much And Forget to Live	NO
Six (6)	Bonds are Strong, The Foundation of our Future	YES
Seven (7)	The Seven Best Wishes of Love, Dreams and Inspiration	YES
Eight (8)	Feeling unfulfilled and abandoned Time to let go of what holds you back	MAYBE
Nine (9)	The Ultimate Wish Card The future is bright	YES
Ten (10)	Pleasant Surprises and Exciting Times Fulfilment and Contentment	YES

Elizabeth Melo, MHs. M

A Quick Recap On Clubs

The following is a quick reference Guide to the meaning of each card in the Clubs Suit. It is important to read the full meanings of each card first, and to use this as a point of reference only.

Ace (A)	Gifts, Achievements, Rewards Distinctive Talent and Inventive Mind	YES
Two (2)	Communication, Focus, Laying the Ground Work towards Goals	MAYBE
Three (3)	The Choice Presents to flourish: Move forward or Remain Stuck	YES
Four (4)	Moving, Security, Balance Time to Rest and Replenish	MAYBE
Five (5)	Masks to be revealed, Secrets to be Unveiled, Maintaining Balance	NO
Six (6)	Sexuality, Intimacy, Approach life with Grace and Diplomacy our Future	MAYBE
Seven (7)	The Unforeseen, Obstacles Persist with Dedication to Succeed	NO
Eight (8)	Gambler's Card, Luck, Eventful A Time of Reward through Diligence	YES
Nine (9)	Overall Wealth Wealth of the Heart, Soul and Material	YES
Ten (10)	Unexpected Sum of Money, Financial Increase, Security	YES

A Quick Recap On Diamonds

The following is a quick reference Guide to the meaning of each card in the Diamonds Suit. It is important to read the full meanings of each card first, and to use this as a point of reference only.

Ace (A)	A Gift, Reward, Stability Material Gains through Efforts	YES
Two (2)	Balance is key, Prudence Be mindful of finances	NO
Three (3)	Accomplishments, Investments Success through Personal Effort	YES
Four (4)	Indecision, Paralyzed by Fear and divorced from Reality	MAYBE
Five (5)	Journey, Frontward or Backwards Choosing Direction	YES
Six (6)	Fertility, Growth, Birth Generosity will be rewarded	YES
Seven (7)	Expect Delays, Patience Retreat to Fight another Day	NO
Eight (8)	Health, Possible Financial Loss Time for Nourishing the Soul	NO
Nine (9)	Advancement, Promises of Success Promotions and Security	YES
Ten (10)	Completion, Success, Buried Treasure Fated for Greatness	YES

Elizabeth Melo, MHs. M

A Quick Recap On Spades

The following is a quick reference Guide to the meaning of each card in the Spades Suit. It is important to read the full meanings of each card first, and to use this as a point of reference only.

Ace (A)	The End, Death, Transformation Loss and Dramatic Change	NO
Two (2)	Stalemate, Vigilance, Deceit, Lies, Opposing Forces Block Our Path	MAYBE
Three (3)	Choice, Separation, Duplicity Betrayal and Emotional Loss	NO
Four (4)	Legal Issues, Legal Papers, Ceasefire, Negotiate, Call a Truce	YES
Five (5)	The Dark Night of the Soul Shall Pass Bittersweet Recovery, Transformation	YES
Six (6)	Conflict, Discord, Disappointment, Quarrels, Stormy Waters Lie Ahead	MAYBE
Seven (7)	Mental Clarity after Strife, A time to Strategize, Theft or Hurdles	YES
Eight (8)	Turmoil, Incarceration, Explosive Energy, State of Mind	NO
Nine (9)	Despair, Suffering, Gossip, Isolation, Paranoia, A Self-imposed Prison	NO
Ten (10)	Overburdened, Overwhelmed, Jealousy Trapped by Our Own Demise	NO

A Quick Recap On Court Cards

The following is a quick reference Guide to the meaning of each Court card in the all of the different Suits. Use this as a Guide only on your journey.

Hearts ♥
Light to medium hair,
or dirty blond or light brown

Jack (J)	Cupids Arrow, Fertility, Invitations	News of a pregnancy, or a significant news	YES
Queen (Q)	Compassion, Intuition, Moodiness	Fluctuating situations, and shadowed truths	YES
King (K)	Spiritual Nature, Advisor, Introspection	Divine intervention, hidden forces that are at work	MAYBE

Clubs ♣
Medium to dark hair, and fair complexion

Jack (J)	Impulsive, Spontaneous	Travel or a sudden change	NO
Queen (Q)	Passionate, Leadership, Bold Action	New energy, open to new experiences	MAYBE
King (K)	Dynamic, Confident, Reckless	Advancement, and good advice, power in action	YES

Elizabeth Melo, MHs. M

Diamonds ♦
Fair or reddish tint of hair
and freckly fair complexion

Jack (J)	Patient, Slow and Steady, Honor	Sudden unexpected communication	YES
Queen (Q)	Practical, Reliable, Worthy	Journey and achievement through hard work	YES
King (K)	Loyal, Devoted, Stability	Advancement at work, promotion and increase in finances	MAYBE

Spades ♠
Dark hair and rich Complexed

Jack (J)	Spontaneous, Charming, Intellectual	Let intellect rule, as opposed to the heart.	MAYBE
Queen (Q)	Independent, Unpredictable, Keen Minded	See endeavors through to the end for success	NO
King (K)	Friendly, Loyal, Fair Minded Bored	encounter with a man in uniform, law or position of power	NO

Spreads and How to Read Them

After learning the meaning of the cards, use the reference guides to help you recall their full meanings, you can now start practicing with the different spreads.

Here you will learn to read *The Celtic Cross, Past – Present – Future Spread, The Magic Square, The Pyramid and The Quick Question Spread*. I will outline the spreads, and how each card ties into the next and its general meaning.

As with all spreads, take your time and explore any other possible angles you might take from a spread. Nothing is written in stone and your own comfort is what counts.

*Discover the enchantment of how
the cards play together and have fun!*

The **Celtic Cross** Spread is perhaps the most traditional spread, and world renowned. It is the bread & butter of spreads and is loaded with tradition.

The **Magic Square** Spread is perhaps the easiest spread to learn aside from the Quick Question Spread. It's a good place to start if you want to get some basic answers and vibe for the cards.

The **Past – Present – Future** Spread is more in-depth and is a great opportunity to see how the past influences the present and affects the future.

The *Pyramid* Spread is more complexed and is best to learn the other spreads before attempting to read it, as it requires focus and ability to really tie the cards together.

The *Quick Question* Spread provides an easy way to ask a question and assess the answer. It's also an easy way to get to know the cards. You can use this spread for Daily readings.

Celtic Cross Spread

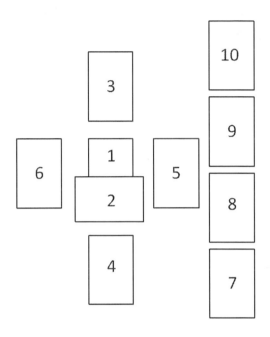

Position 1: Covering Card

This card signifies the situation that is currently surrounding
the seeker's life, what is happening, or
how the Seeker feels in the current moment.

Position 2: Crossing Card

This card shows the present conflict or the problem. It may
not be negative card, but is still a challenge to be faced.

Position 3: Crowning Card

This card reflects the general atmosphere and the biggest
influence in the seekers life. It represents goals or desires, and is
the general feeling of where they stand at the present moment.

Elizabeth Melo, MHs. M

Position 4: Base of the Matter, the Secret Card

This card represents the unknown element or unknown influence and could indicate a sudden unexpected force that is not anticipated, this is a surprise affecting the situation.

Position 5: Passing Influence

This card describes what event or person from past is influencing the current affairs. This could help interpret how the seeker reached their current position.

Position 6: Forthcoming Influences

This card describes what is about to manifest in the seeker's life. Here we are given clues into the direction the seeker is taking, should they stay on the current path. The seeker has the option to change this forecast.

Position 7: The Crossroad, How one see our selves

This is the crossroad point in the cards and indicates how the seeker feels and what choices lay ahead. It can reveal their worries, concerns from their own perspective. This can also guide them to what hinders their forward movement.

Position 8: The Views of Others

This card reveals the impact and views of others on the state of affairs. This indicates how your environment perceives you, but also how it affects the situation. We cannot change how we are perceived, only how we perceive ourselves

Position 9: Hopes and Fear

Hopes and Fears can be the same thing, as the duality of human nature is to sometimes fear what we want most. It indicates what we secretly desire, as well as what we fear most related to the situation.

Position 10: Final Outcome

This final position card is an indication of how the present condition will play out should the seeker continue on the same path forecasted by the other cards in the spread, but again free will triumphs destiny, remind the seeker there are always choices.

Magic Square Spread

This spread uses 9 cards in total, but its details are formed through its interconnection. It's a fun and easy spread to learn how to do a general reading, or it can be useful in asking questions.

Position 5: The Heart of the Matter

Positions 1, 2 and 3: Past influences related to the question,

Positions 4, 5 and 6: The present mood or situation

Positions 7, 8 and 9: The future possibilities

Once you have the general essence of the spread from positions 1 through 9, you can begin reading the lines in other directions for details, hints, guidance and understanding. There are so many possibilities with this spread, enjoy it and play with it, explore its hidden messages.

Past – Present – Future Spread

Each row represents the past, present and future. It indicates what part of the past is currently affecting the present, and what the future will hold should the seeker continue on this path. This spread uses 21 cards. The spread itself can be very detailed and tell several different stories that you can explore for guidance.

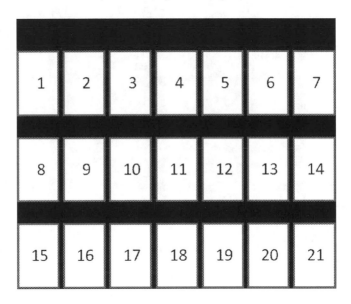

Past: Cards 1 to 7
The Past circumstances that lead to the present.

Present: Card 8 to 14
The present circumstances or passing influence.

Future: Card 15 to 21
The final outcome will be if the seeker stays on their current path.

**Reading the Lines Vertically**

Interpret each vertical line by taking the centre card, and linking it to the past and future for additional insight into the current situation. For example: read Card 8, and see how it relates to Cards 1 and 15 and do this throughout.

Pyramid Spread

The Pyramid is a complex spread with various rows and triangles each telling a different story to encompass the most important points related to our current affairs and potential outcomes.

Before you begin to decipher the spread, take a few moments to review its essence. How many of the same suit or numbers do you see, and what does it tell you?

Once you have done that, read the largest Pyramid first with Position 1 as the ultimate influence, and bear this knowledge throughout the reading.

Take notice that there are four more triangles inside the larger Pyramid. The top triangle is the forefront of the reading and most important, it is the heart of the matter, and what is more important to the seeker.

Elizabeth Melo, MHs. M

The three triangles at the bottom should be read separately with each triangle telling its own story. The story it tells maybe separate from the overall reading. It might indicate a side story regarding something else close to the seeker. For example, one triangle might be regarding career while another might be regarding matters of the heart. Take heed to break them down and tell each story, after all our lives our multifaceted and contains many dimensional aspects and components.

Once you have determined each triangle, begin reading each line from the bottom upwards. The bottom is the base of the matter, indicating the past influences that are affecting the present.

The second line from the bottom determines the present situation and what is most important to the seeker at this time.

The middle row, third from the bottom, is indicating more than one possible outcome, and presents the seeker with the choices they will face.

The fourth row from the bottom, are the cards that determine what will come of the situation if the seeker continues on the current path.

The final crowning card determines the final and overall essence of the reading.

The heart of man is very much like the sea,
it has its storms,
it has its tides
and in its depths it has its pearls too
~ Vincent van Gogh

Quick Question Spread

This is an easy quick spread designed to be read for specific questions. This spread is very easy and it is a great way to help you practice using the cards and studying their meanings. This spread is a wonderful tool for Daily Readings, and might help guide you along your day to day life.

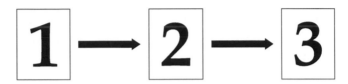

This 3 (three) card spread provides a simple overview of life along with answers for direct questions. It presents the questions as in its present state, and highlights the past influence, and the possible outcome.

Start by shuffling the cards the same as you would any other spread. Cut the deck twice, forming 3 piles. The cards should be face down. Take the top card and flip it over to reveal which cards have unfolded.

Another way that some readers perform this spread is by fanning the cards across the table face down and picking out 3 cards, or in the case of a seeker, they can choose their own 3 cards.

In the descriptions available for each suit, you will find that they provide a *YES, NO, MAYBE* answer. This is a great time to refer to the reference guide to offer you some insight.

The Centre card represents the current conditions, while the card to the left implicates the past influence to the question, and the final card to the right reveals the likely outcome.

Final Words ... Remember!

The following examples are actual readings that I have personally given. Direct references have been replaced to respect the privacy of my clients. Ultimately with each of the following examples, I provide a summary of my personal assessment on the reading.

Please bear in mind which each spread, that I am guided by my instincts, and that the meaning of the spread may be different depending on the person.

My deepest wish is that this will help you along your journey to learning the art of Cartomancy, or at least provide you with personal insight and guidance.

I highly encourage that you keep a dairy of your own readings, as I suggested earlier on, and include the dates and a brief summary. Down the road you will enjoy reviewing the readings and finding the connection with your actual life. This will be useful in learning and also fun and engaging.

I have enjoyed my time writing these pages, and hope that you have enjoyed the journey thus far, and that your will revel in your own readings, find guidance and perhaps even become a reader yourself.

Namaste

For me, this is my absolute truth,
living by the words of true greatness....

Gandhi once said:
"In a gentle way, you can shake the world."

And he also said
"Love is the strongest force the world possesses."

So true

Elizabeth Melo, MHs. M

Example of A Celtic Cross Reading

When you first look at the spread, its dominating suit is Hearts, which indicates that the seeker is most concerned or focused on matters of the heart, and emotional needs. With 10's repeating twice in a 10 card spread, the seeker is closing chapters in her life, saying good-bye to the old, and is ready to move in a new direction. However, with Hearts being prevalent, it indicates that an end of a relationship is still affecting her, and although it appears to have been in the past it is she is holding to her fears.

Position 1: Here in this position is the seeker herself, as she is represented by the Queen of Clubs, she is a Medium Haired woman, with a fair eyes and complexion. Finding her in this position indicates that she is fully committed to finding her happiness and well-being, but may need to be reminded that there is a world outside that needs her attention as well.

Position 2: The 8 of Clubs in position 2, indicates that she is experiencing a change in luck, and the status quo is transforming. However, in this particular position it conveys an issue as this is the crossing card, and therefore this card should be interpreted that her good fortune may also lead to over indulgence and irresponsibility. This is a good time to gentle remind the seeker to stay focused on her dreams and wishes, and to place herself in check. She is not selfish in this case, but she may be investing too much of her time in frivolous activities.

Position 3: 10 of hearts is the crowning card and it suggests that she is focused on her happiness, and this card is one of great optimism and likely her happiness will present soon. This is the buffer card, soon she is heading into a time in her life that the past will not matter. She is gaining confidence and she is enthusiastic about her future. However with 8 of Clubs in the preceding position, there is great potential, but she should be reminded of the expression "easy come, easy go", and as quickly as her good fortune is here, she should exercise caution and prioritize her responsibilities.

Position 4: With the Jack of Spades in this position, personally I view it as a younger man entering the seekers life. He would be younger than her, and have dark hair and darker skin. He is a sudden appearance, and he is connecting to matters of the heart indicating a romantic relationship. (This is how I chose to see it, however, this card could also speak to childish behavior and her irresponsibility.

See what I mean, you need to use your instincts to decide. For me this represents a younger man.)

Position 5: The 5 of clubs in the position representing the passing influence. Here, we find that she has been betrayed in her past on a romantic level, and considering the circumstances and essence of her cards. It conveys the message that she is afraid to open her heart and being hurt again. This may explain why she is in a state of fear and irresponsibility. It's always good to bear in mind the feelings of your seeker, and in this case gentle explain to her that you understand that she has hurt and betrayal in her past, but urge her to let go, and move on to the brightness that is presenting in her cards.

Position 6: The 2 of Hearts is indicating a relationship that is new and exciting soon entering her life, and may even be in the present, as indicated by the Jack of Spades but definitely a more recent development. This card indicates there is great potential for happiness, but she should heed the warning of the cards, as she may be blinded by her fear, and therefore react badly to anything she could interpret as a slight, real or imagined.

Position 7: The 5 of hearts is sitting in the cross road of the seekers life, and aligns perfectly with the situation indicated by the other cards. She is experiencing a time of evaluating her life, she is in the soul searching stages, and is trying to 'figure it out'. This tells us that she has already come through the dark night of the soul, she is no longer in rock bottom and is trying to figure out her future, what she truly wants, and what truly makes her happy.

Position 8: This is how others may perceive her and her behavior. In this position we find the Joker and explains that those around her feel she is erratic and emotionally unclear. In denotes a time when those closest to her are concerned and those that are of less importance in her life, may consider her an emotional wreck. This card also further implicates her over indulgence state of mind and her behavior is not promoting her best interests at heart.

Position 9: This is representing her hopes and fears with the 6 of Hearts. This tells us that she is searching for love, and down deep inside she craves settling down, and being in a committed relationship. However, what she wants most she is afraid of, and she is finding it difficult to let go and trust in love. She may also be afraid that she will never find her true love again.

Position 10: As a final outcome is the Ace of Hearts. This is a very positive card and especially in this position. This tells us that her wishes can be found, but with the Ace of Hearts, it doesn't come without effort. She should be encouraged to face her fears, be true to her heart, and open her mind to the opportunities. She need only apply herself, reach out and grab it, and she will have everything she dreams to have. This is a good time for the 5 of Hearts to appear in Position 7, as her soul searching is leading her to great happiness and renewed hope

Example of A Magic Square Reading

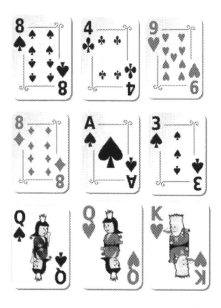

I would like to start this spread by expressing that this reading was particularly hard and I chose it so that you, as a potential reader, can understand the scope of how things can sometimes be difficult to express. If you should find yourself in a similar situation, my advice is to tread lightly, and be extremely gentle when delivering this kind of reading.

The predominating implication of the cards is a *NO*, in terms of a question. However with the 9 of Hearts present in the spread, there is a strong *MAYBE* hinted here. My personal interpretation is that the seeker may get her wish, but not as she wished it. This is clearly a moment for evaluation, and the adage "be careful what you wish for, you just might get it" comes to mind. Things are not black and white, and there are hidden secrets that she does not know, and she herself is hiding her true motivations.

The cards express distinctively that that she is involved in an affair situation, and for sure she is the other woman. Her hope is that she will win the heart of the man she wants who is married or otherwise committed to another. As she appears as the Queen of Spades and closer to him is the Queen of Hearts. This is a complicated situation.

She may continue this affair in its current state, but her hope to one day have a fully committed relationship with this man would not be in the cards for her. She will never fully have what she desires unless she chooses to search for love in another direction. The choice will be hers, as this is her free will. At this point, she is not only betraying herself, but she is betraying the situation. After all, she is carrying on with a committed man, and is playing the happy devoted other woman to his face, and all the while she seethes beneath the surface. To be truly happy, and fulfilled she is advised to walk away. Otherwise she will remain stuck in a relationship that will never give her all that she desires, and will only infuriate her insecurities.

The other big warning is the 8 of Spades which not only falls in the cards but directly to her, it's a clear indication that she is not thinking straight, and she may be prone to explosive outbursts. She is warned to keep herself in check, especially since she can make the situation even worse. All round this is not a positive situation, and she is at the point where her heart is not truly committed any more, and yet she feels competitive to remain so that she can be the victor.

The overtone of her state of mind is not healthy. She is dangerously close to becoming unhinged. It is unmistakable that she is the maker of her own demise, and yet she saunters forward with little regard for the heart of everyone involved, including her own fragile heart. She is too unstable to see things clearly. She should be guided towards redeeming herself by walking away, or minimally re-evaluating how she truly feels, as in this case her love is fading, and she is no longer holding on for true love, but for her ego and her need be the *champion*.

Guide her towards seeking out guidance from either friends or even better, get some counselling. Sadly this is a dark time for the seeker. As the reader, I was very gentle and focused on her finding her true motivation, and spiritual self.

Example of
Past – Present – Future Spread

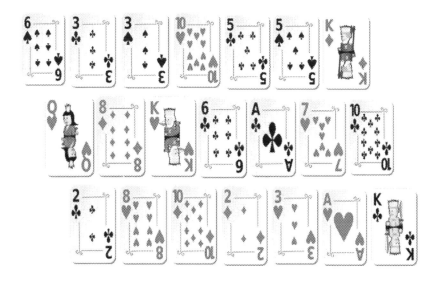

What do you see and how do you feel when you see this spread? The overall predominant suit is Clubs. This indicates that the reading is focused on personal ambitions, deepest desires and a need for recognition. The seeker should be reminded to re-evaluated his own self-worth, and be less preoccupied with the views of others. It also suggests that the seeker is more motivated by security in life than by emotions and love. He would do well to remember that happiness is more than just security, and the need for security can lead to repeating bad decisions. Balance is the key here. The numbers that repeat the most are 3's, K's and 10's. There is a strong indication of rough changes with 3's repeating, however with the 10's, it indicate that the seeker can trust that the end is near, and new beginning will come soon. Also indicated with the K's is that important meetings are taking place that will bring the seeker good fortune. The Seeker himself is present as the Kind of Clubs, and he is medium hair, with fair complexion, and blue eyed.

The First Row: Indicates past influences, and in this case there has been bitter arguments, betrayal and end of a relationship. The ties are severing here, and the end of the relationship has occurred. Over all the betrayal seems to have been an affair and there is heartbreak, and devastation in the past. It also indicates that the seeker has been in a dark place for some time, perhaps in a depression, or unstable state of mind. However, the 10 of Hearts present in the Spread is a positive omen, and in this particular position of the past, it promises that the seeker will head in the right direction and overcome a bad break up, and heart ache, and will come out on top of the situation. If the breakup has already occurred, which may be very likely in the position of the past, the seeker is still reminiscent, healing on some level, and struggling to let go.

The Second Row: Indicates the present circumstances where the seeker finds himself positioned at the current moment. There are several tidbits here to consider. First there is a health alert, and the seeker should consider: what is he doing that may not be good for him? What is causing him stress? Has he been taking care of his physical and mental self? There is a possible alert for someone close around the seeker, and for me, my instinct suggest the light hair woman present in the cards may be suffering a small illness, and is someone close to the seeker. He may hear unfavorable news regarding this woman health. I also see that there is a new sexual partner entering the seekers life in the form of a light to medium haired man. This could lead to a wonderful fulfilling relationship, but no promise is indicated by the cards at this time. This suggests that the seeker should not ricochet straight into another relationship and allow time to fully heal from the past. If the seeker allows himself to "go with the flow" he will triumph over his status quo, and find fulfilment. There is also an indication that a small lump of money may fall into his lap, or at least something of monetary value.

The Third Row: Open communication will lead to celebration. If the seeker continues on this current path, he will come full circle. His wishes will present eventually, he needs only reach out to grab them. Money, or financial increases seem quite significant, however, the two of diamonds indicates that the seeker lives life continually concerned about finances and this could hinder his own joy and happiness in life. He should lighten up and re-evaluate what really will bring him complete and utter bliss. The seeker will find love again, once he has figured out his priorities, and it will be strong and promising. The King of Clubs, the seeker himself, in the final position implies that he will complete the cycle, but he needs to consider who does he want to be when it's all been said and done. Answering this question will bring him to his destination. He should be guided to relax, and breath in the greatness of the moment, and the coming influences, and concern himself less with the monetary, or security. After all what is life without a little risk, and an open heart?

Other little bits of information when you read top to bottom is also relevant. In this spread we see the seeker may have an argument or upsetting conversation with a light haired woman. It also says that the severing of ties led the seeker into unhealthy behavior; however, he is in a time of renewing himself again. It also re-enforces the seeker should not repeat mistakes by entering into a relationship with security as the priority he should have fun and enjoy the experience. There is a definite air of overcoming the past, and the potential for great success. The seeker can in essence, or as they say, 'have it all'. This is truly up to him. Let go of the past and learn to live in the moment. The lesson here is that you cannot give from an empty cup. He should be encouraged to focus on feeding his soul, in a healthy

Elizabeth Melo, MHs. M

and productive way, so that when he is ready his cup will be full, and then he can be truly happy.

Always remember, what others think of us is not a sincere reflection of who we are. Hold one face, be true and authentic!

Example of
A Pyramid Spread

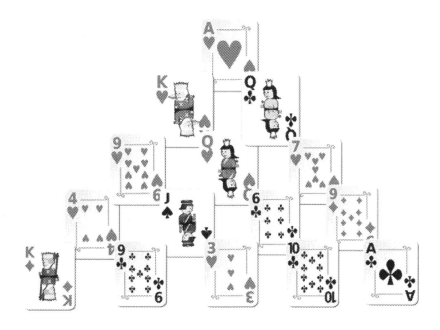

This is a larger spread to interpret, but this particular flow is quite lovely, I could not help myself to share it. This spread is an easy read, if you look closely. The predominant suit in the spread is hearts with seven out of 15 cards. There are also five Clubs therefore it showcases that matters of the heart are the main desires and concerns, but aspects of her goals and ambitions are highlighted and will play an important role in her spread. Clearly indicated that the most important quality she seeks is love!

You will also notice that Kings and Queen's and Ace's are repeating, and the most important repeat is three 9's present! It's easy to see that this is a busy spread. First and foremost are the matters of the heart.

Elizabeth Melo, MHs. M

She is represented by the Queen of Clubs, and with the surrounding cards we see that she is a smart and talented woman. While the Kings and Queen's repeating suggesting reunions, gatherings and celebration, and the Ace's bear the message that new beginnings are already presenting, and good changes are coming her way.

The important repeat of 9's gives us a sense of her living for the moment inside herself, lost in thought, and redefining herself as a woman. She craves changes, not only in the exterior world, but within. She has the power to manifest all her dreams, once she has passed through this period of definition and characterizing herself again, as a woman of strength and self-worth. Her priorities have changed, she is venturing into a time of taking what she wants as she wants it and becoming more in tuned with herself and what she truly wants. With the 9 of Hearts specifically tells us that her wishes are coming true. The overall spread is joyful and happy.

Crowning the Cards is the Ace of Hearts, a good omen that promotes a time to pursue her dreams and make them a reality. As you can see she has both the 9 of Hearts and the Ace of Hearts, which is an ultimate combination for any wishes she is holding, not to mention that in the spread itself we have the 9 of Clubs, a card of overall wealth, wealth of heart, wealth of soul and financial security. At an overview of the spread the cards are laying in a positive way, and the seeker can expect a positive turn of events. There is definitely an up-swing in her life.

The top Triangle shows the anticipation of love and romance being highlighted as the strongest expression of her cards, and it states that her ultimate wishes lay with love and commitment and she herself, represented by the Queen of Clubs is standing next to her wishes. However, note that she and the King of Hearts appear to have their backs to each other, and there is a Queen of Hearts between them, and the Queen of Hearts is showing a great interest in this man.

Although in saying this, it is noteworthy to say his back is falling to her as well. Despite this, for him to appear in the top triangle, he is still significant, and appears to hold feelings for the seeker. His choice to walk away from her appears confusing and unjust. This begs the question why are they not together? It is perplexing and difficult to understand his motivation. The first initial feeling that I had was that he was not ready for a full-on commitment and was afraid of how he felt about the seeker, and she confirmed that he in fact was in the middle of a divorce, and was still struggling with the end of his marriage. This makes sense to the reading.

When we look at the overall spread, the first thing that popped into focus was that both wish cards fall in the same row to two men, the King of Hearts as well as the King of Diamonds. You might ask how this can be, but it's easy to see that she still as deep feelings for the King of Hearts. However, she is showing renewed strength, and still remains hopeful and with an open heart. This spread clearly displays the arrival of a new man coming into her life, the King of Diamonds, and it will be a relationship of significance and undoubtedly impact the future events to come. The presence of the 3 of Spades insinuates that she will be the one faced with a choice between both men, as it indicates that at some point the King of Hearts will return to her expecting to pick up where they left off.

Notice that the King of Diamonds also falls to some lovely cards aside from the wishes. It is indicated that he is a successful man, and a man of a certain wealth. He appears as a person open to a new relationship, and appears uncomplicated, or unattached at this time. Therefore she could easily accept this invitation into a new relationship. The King of Diamonds is appearing at a time in her life, where she is alone and open to possibilities. The reappearance of the King of Hearts will certainly give her pause, there was a strong bond between them and she will find it difficult to face the choice between the two men, and discover where her heart truly lays. The

King of Hearts has already hurt her, yet her feelings for him are still strong, however, before this the King of Hearts has gathered his strength and re-appears in her life, she will have invested enough time in the King of Diamonds for him to matter and feelings will have developed between them, and therefore she will be caught in a love triangle, where the decision of whom she chooses will be up to her. Notice that around her career cards romance is falling and this may imply that she could meet the King of Diamonds somewhere along her career path, and may in fact meet him soon, or even have cross paths with him at some point. There will be an immediate attraction for her.

This bring us to the second most significant aspect of her cards, which without a doubt brings her great success in business or career. She is seen as an outstanding woman and highly intelligent, who is held in high regard in her career. There is a strong indication that she will receive an award of some sort and be recognized for an achievement. This award will lead her further down the career path by opening even more opportunities in her future. This is a woman who will achieve her goals and beyond them. There is also a chance that her achievements may make her famous on some level. She is a driving force, with a brilliant mind.

As a side note, her back seems to be turned to a man from her past. He is showing as a younger man with a rich complexion, represented by the Jack of Spades. He appears to be involved with another woman, but as the cards indicate with the 6 of Clubs, his interests seem to be purely sexual in both herself and the other woman. He comes across as immature, needy and vain. She is right to turn her back to him, as this situation will never be one that will bring her happiness and fulfillment. His appearance indicates that he will continue to attempt sexual advances towards her, for this is foolish young man, who seems to fancy himself a Greek god.

Overall, this spread is one that is positive and enlightening. The seeker will find herself at the cross roads sooner then expected, and although she will face big decision that impact her life for a long time to come, she is on the road to happiness, contentment and peace of mind. She is truly a warrior and a champion of her own life.

"True love cannot be found where it does not exist,
nor can it be hidden where it truly does."
~ William Shakespeare

Example of
A Quick Question Spread

What do you see, and what do the cards tell you? What is your first initial vibe? I may have chosen an easy decipher here, for that reason, I have chosen to include two samples, so that you can have a different perspective.

The seeker asked the question regarding a new business venture that he was undertaking and he was feeling unsure about his next steps. He questioned whether or not he should gamble more time and money to advancing the mission, or should he retreat and consider another option. Clearly he was feeling self-doubt and apprehensive.

The cards in this small spread were so adamant that the answer was **YES**, that the seeker should not abandon his project, but move forward fully committed and resume his energy. This was 100% in his favour. It was also indicative with the 9 of Diamonds appearing in the spread that he would also find assistance and guidance to help him move forward in his venture. Good advice will be given, and the seeker will succeed. The only thing that could stand in his way is his own trepidation.

Another Example of
A Quick Question Spread

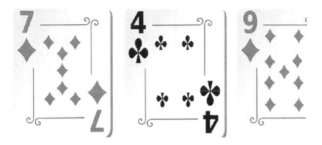

The seekers question was related to career and advancement. Her hope was to be promoted to the next level. She had an air of one who had already had some great successes behind her life due to her dedication. She seemed self-confident, and genuine.

The answer is unclear in this case, with a *YES, NO and MAYBE* represented. However, in looking closely at the meanings of the cards, my personal interpretation led me to conclude that the answer is likely *YES*.

Now I know you are asking why, so let me explain. The 9 of Diamonds is a career card, and the 7 of Diamonds is a delay card. From this alone I drew the conclusion that she will advance in her career, however she will experience unexpected delays, as things will not happen in the immediate future or in the timeframe she is hoping. The other noteworthy card is the 4 of Clubs, which indicates movement, that is a positive reflection on the question as well and my immediate reaction was she would relocate as part of her advancement. The advice in the cards as I interpret them is she should adopt the motto *"good things come to those who wait"*, and the outcome will be one that she is waiting for and she will reap the rewards for years to come.

Highlights of My Life

I once read cards for a man who seemed to have some respiratory problems, but health was coming through strong in his spread. I told him of my concerns, and he felt that due to his respiratory problems that it was obvious and dismissed it immediately. However, I could not let this go, I closed my eyes, and focused with all my might, and I could feel something in the lower abdominal area. I encouraged this man to seek a health professional, and told him it was something significant. He eventually followed my advice, and discovered that he had bowel cancer but he was still in the operational stages, and was lucky to have discovered the problem so early on.

I recall doing cards for a very young woman, a mother of one, and in a relationship. She was barely 20 years old. What I could see and also feel from her is that she had exceptionally low self-esteem. Her self-confidence was totally shattered, and she was meek and fearful. I could feel that on some level she was abused, not only by her relationship, but growing up around bully's and an unhealthy family dynamic. Her self-esteem was grounded so deep inside her, from years of being told she was not smart, not good enough, and the proverbial loser. It was hard to look into the face of this terrified young woman and watch her drown. Would she really listen to anything I had to say? She was smart, and I could see great potential. I told her that I could see her advancing her education, and that she would do very well, she need only apply herself. She told me that she knew she was stupid, and could never achieve anything. I was stunned, and actually angry, not at her of course, but at all the people that had shattered her, drowned her in this pit hole and kept her there. But I stood my ground, told her I knew better and knew of her potential. A few years went by, and my brother, who taught at a local college, said that he had a student, who told him that she had met me, and that because of me, she decided to change her life. My brother told me she was in the top of her class. I was filled with pride.

I have tears in my eyes just writing this. For all the times that I thought about giving up doing readings for people either because of my ego or insecurities, I remember moments like this, where I helped, and was detrimental in encouraging their well-being. I was gifted, so how could I give this up? I realized it was my ego, and that I did not want to be seen as a charlatan, a fake person, who sputtered off words to feed her pocket. That was not me! I was kind and honest, and obviously somewhat concerned with her image and insecure in her talent.

Silly me!

These are just a couple of moments in my life, but there are so many times that I was able to help others perceive themselves differently, encourage them from depression, gave them hope and the ability to dream again. Being a reader comes with a foundation of solid moral ethics, but more importantly, a good councillor, and warm heart.

To be seen as a gifted and special person by my clients throughout the years, has given me strength, to keep reading, sharing my knowledge and helping those who seek my guidance through their trials and tribulations. For that I am both honored and grateful.

I was at my own cross-roads, but I have finally chosen to embrace who I truly am, not only my gifts, but to gift them to others. I believe that this is my destiny.

"It is not in the stars to hold our destiny,
but in ourselves"
~ William Shakespeare

Elizabeth Melo, MHs. M

Special thanks to the following people for contribution:

Jason Brace for his friendship, edits and constant encouragement, you are a rock star.
CJ Anstey who provided some of the bones in this book, though she has passed on now, I hope she has found peace and that she knows her wisdom will live on.
To all my family and friends who believed in me, and encouraged me to move forward when I was filled with doubts, how many times have you all said, just do it!!!!
I'm here now, doing it!
Know that you are the anchor to my ship!

As very special thank you to my clients, who after all these years have stood by me, and looked for my guidance.
Thank you for believing in me!
I am both honoured and humbled, and so very grateful.

And finally to two special men in my life who have passed on:
My father, who taught me to bear an open mind, and that the truth is how you perceive things,
and my brother, who picked my brain from a very early age, our conversations over a pot of coffee,
on pyramids, ancient text, divinations, reincarnation, astrology religion, God, Gia, Goddess and on and on…..
I should have listened to you years ago, and followed my destiny.

Printed in the United States
By Bookmasters